D0190539

d to any bran...
...n or before the date

How to Be English

HOW TO BE
ENGLISH

. . . in 100 objects, occasions and peculiarities

DAVID BOYLE

■ SQUARE PEG

1 3 5 7 9 10 8 6 4 2

Square Peg, an imprint of Vintage,
20 Vauxhall Bridge Road,
London SW1V 2SA

Square Peg is part of the Penguin Random House group of companies
whose addresses can be found at global.penguinrandomhouse.com.

Penguin
Random House
UK

First published by Square Peg in 2015

www.vintage-books.co.uk

A CIP catalogue record for this book is available
from the British Library

ISBN 9780224100977

Text Design by Lindsay Nash

Typeset by Palimpsest Book Production Ltd, Falkirk, Stirlingshire

Printed and bound by Clays Ltd, St Ives plc

Penguin Random House is committed to a sustainable future for our
business, our readers and our planet. This book is made from Forest
Stewardship Council® certified paper.

In memory of my wonderful grandparents

CONTENTS

INTRODUCTION

'Dinner was announced soon after our arrival, which consisted of the following things,' wrote Rev. James Woodforde describing his meal on 20 April 1796, in a diary which – in a very English way – describes food in great detail but barely mentions God at all. Then he takes a deep breath and sets out the table before him:

> Salmon boiled & Shrimp Sauce, some White Soup, Saddle of Mutton rosted & Cucumber &c., Lambs Fry, Tongue, Breast of Veal ragoued, rice Pudding the best part of a Rump of Beef stewed immediately after the Salmon was removed. 2nd course. A Couple of Spring Chicken, rosted Sweetbreads, Jellies, Maccaroni, frill'd Oysters, 2 small Crabs, & made Dish of Eggs . . . We got home about half past nine, as we went very slowly on Account of Briton's walking, who . . . was very imprudent indeed, but I believe he had been making too free with Mr Mellishs Beer &c.

There is a glimpse here, perhaps, of the soul of the English. We have a culture like a rummage sale, like a white-elephant stall, hideously divided and bizarrely coherent – and, over the last century or so, obscured by an even more varied invention known as 'Britishness'. The British have a terrible reputation for cuisine, but the English have a different reputation: for overindulgence, and plain, gargantuan portions.

That is the way the English used to eat, and I have a feeling they would do again, given the chance. There is a little of the overindulgent eighteenth century in all of us. Perhaps not in our genes; there are so many people here – and always have been – from other parts of the world. With the best will in the world, there is no way they can share the particular mixed English genetic heritage. Nor is it quite the English environment and weather which we all share that shapes us, because the weather has changed from the heat of the twelfth century to the frost fairs on the Thames of the eighteenth.

No, it must be something else – some other historical imperative, some psychic beating of the traditional heart of the land – perched on the far north-west corner of Europe, peering out towards the west. Something shapes the English – it does not homogenise them, which would not be English at all – but it makes them stand out, whether they like it or not, whether they are from the backstreets of Karachi or the tiny Jewish villages of old Poland. We can't know what that is, but we can look at the flotsam and jetsam of history that amount to the whole.

This book that you hold in your hand tries to gather up some of those strands. As such, it is both a celebration and investigation of Englishness and an instruction manual for those who might like to be more English. It is also a guidebook for those of us who are not absolutely sure who we are.

And the confusion is only reasonable. The English themselves are a pretty diverse bunch and there are many different kinds of English people, even among the same social strata. Take the two great English heroes of the Napoleonic era, Nelson and Wellington (Nelson was from Norfolk, though Wellington was, strictly speaking, Irish). They only met once, in the lobby of the Colonial Office in Downing Street, shortly before the Battle of Trafalgar in 1805. They disliked each other on sight. Wellington said Nelson was 'vain and silly'; Nelson didn't survive long enough to write about his own feelings. It was only because Lord Castlereagh kept them waiting for three quarters of an hour that there was any kind of meeting of minds.

This misunderstanding is usually explained in terms of a difference in career and timing. Nelson was at the height of his fame and Wellington, then Sir Arthur Wellesley, was not yet a national hero, and he felt ignored and patronised by the little one-eyed, one-armed admiral. But there is another way of looking at why they annoyed each other. Because although they represented the same nation, they could not have had more contrasting personalities, And because Wellington virtually invented the new 'British' personality, adding to the traditional English reputation for phlegm a whole new veneer that was all his own – tight-lipped, unemotional, clipped.

'My God, I've lost my leg!' shouted the Earl of Uxbridge, later Marquess of Anglesey, next to Wellington at Waterloo, after a cannon-ball carried it away at the height of battle.

Wellington glanced down, unsurprised and unrelenting. 'By God, sir,' he said. 'So you have.'

Nelson, on the other hand, was easily a match for Wellington for his strategic genius and personal bravery, but he represented a much more old-fashioned personality – emotional, overindulgent, senti-mental, lachrymose, and overwhelmingly English. Wellington was never any of those. No wonder they disliked each other to start with.

So what is it to be English? Is it by turning a Nelsonian blind eye to authority or is it the Wellingtonian stiff upper lip? Is it a senti-mental attachment to animals, is it a fondness for some of the most magnificently horrible vegetables on the planet, is it a nostalgic regard for tradition, or is it our love both of the monarchy and of the underdog? Probably it is a mixture of all these things.

These are increasingly urgent questions. The Scots and Welsh are clear about who they are, and are aware of themselves as nations in the United Kingdom. Their demands for self-determination are, to some extent, being met. They are grown-up countries, not vassals. But who are the English? The Scots have 'Flower of Scotland'; the Welsh have any number of songs including 'Cwm Rhondda' and 'Myfanwy' and 'We'll Keep a Welcome'. The Irish have their own ambiguities, it is true, but what do the English have, except a vague, polite on-the-one-hand-on-the-other-hand?

This is partly because the English have always been polite. The English have always apologised for themselves wherever they go. They like pluck, fair play and cricket. Wimbledon and the Derby still have a place in their hearts, but there are peculiar ways in which they feel most comfortable not winning. They also don't like articulating what they are, in case someone contradicts them. This is partly political correctness – the nation is so diverse, so multi-racial, so contradictory – but it is more than that. They have always expressed themselves and articulated their values in deliberately ambiguous ways – and who can say they are wrong? But it does leave a bit of a gap.

The British Empire has long since disappeared, the Union Jack may go the way of the Union, 'Rule, Britannia' is slightly embarrassing (as the English put it), and the very word 'British' seems to have given way to a crumbling 'United Kingdom', which we all know is not *that* united. The days, a century or more ago, when politicians could blithely use the term 'English' to include everyone on these islands, has now gone.

There has therefore never been a more urgent moment to revive a sense of Englishness, and this book is designed to knit it back together again, contradictory bit by bit.

*

There was another reason for writing the book. I was wandering down Monsal Dale in Derbyshire, the extraordinarily English beauty spot where John Ruskin campaigned against the dramatic viaduct – built, as he put it, 'so that every fool in Buxton can be in Bakewell in half an hour'. The viaduct is now preserved and is part of the amazing network of long-distance footpaths that criss-cross the nation. And as I climbed down to the river below, I found myself wondering how my children would ever learn about the traditional stories and songs which are their heritage.

They are hardly going to learn them in school. The national curriculum endlessly repeats the founding myth of the modern British state – the 1940 invasion that never was – but barely goes otherwise beyond the Tudors and an occasional whiff of the Romans. If they go to Anglican schools, they may get a few traditional hymn tunes, but that is pretty much the limit.

So if they are going to learn anything about being English, I'm going to have to teach them myself. But what should I tell them? Should I sing them 'Polly Oliver', or would they have me locked up? Should I tell them about Robin Hood and the Armada? Should I tell them about Sir John Moore at Corunna and Captain Scott? Should I read them *Children of the New Forest*? Or are these curmudgeonly, backward-looking hangovers from the days of *Downton Abbey*?

Should we still know which clothes are correct for which occasions, and why pinstripe suits exist? Should we extol St George and St George's Day? After all, this sort of English identity can make people nervous.

On one level, this is a manual. It is a book which you could give to a visitor from another planet, and which would given them a complete grounding in the idiosyncracies of the English. It also pins down and captures the absurdities and warmth of Englishness at its best, and why – despite everything – we are rather proud of it. In fact, this is a book that can help us learn to be English all over again. It will show us how by providing, in a way that can be dipped into or read right through, a compendium of the peculiarities and cultural tics that make us English.

And once you set out these little English peculiarities, it is clear how much of a mongrel nation we have always been. So few of those institutions that we call our own are unambiguously English in origin – they have been borrowed from cultures all over the world, just as we have borrowed people from all over the world.

The English have always been a tolerant nation, though it may not have seemed like that if you were a foreign merchant being chased through the backstreets of medieval London by the wild apprentices of the City. They have incorporated and assimilated, not always easily, and not always consciously, and have created a para-doxical, varied culture that seems at the same time to reach back to the past but also to change all the time.

'What should they know of England who only England know?' wrote Rudyard Kipling, urging the strangely insular English to look beyond their shores to where their fellow countrypeople struggled to live, in Calcutta or Lahore or Shanghai or Cairo or Lagos. It is true that, to learn what is most obvious about yourself, you sometimes have to listen to what foreigners say about you.

Evelyn Waugh puts the negative in the voice of Anthony Blanche, the waspish, camp, half-English gossip of *Brideshead Revisited*, a character he based partly on Brian Howard and partly on Harold Acton, who had famously recited T. S. Eliot's *The Waste Land* to the rowing toughs on Christ Church Meadow in Oxford. He warns the hero about charm:

Charm is the great English blight. It does not exist outside these damp islands. It spots and kills anything it touches. It kills love; it kills art; I greatly fear, my dear Charles, it has killed *you*.

This book is full of English charm, so this is a reasonable warning to bear in mind. It is perhaps that the English insist on a stubborn, perhaps lazy, refusal to demand too much for themselves, their determination to live like hobbits: comfortable, bourgeois, unexciting lives – facing up to challenges and extremes which are different from those of other nationalities. But we need to defend the English a little here. Separately, the garden sheds, tree and football worship, nostalgia, and giant, stodgy puddings with custard, may not amount to much. But, taken together, they amount to a civilised way of life, which is constantly changing and yet always the same.

So, with a view to capturing all the rich foibles, traditions and quirks of English culture and history for the next generation, before they are forgotten, I have selected the hundred entries that follow. Everyone in England would probably select different things – that is partly what makes them English – but I hope readers will forgive the personal selection, my own desert-island choices, and use it as a starting point to make their own. And then pass them on.

Key to logos

Monarchy	Food	Fashion
Folklore	Sport	Music
Literature	Seafaring	Nature
Buildings	Tradition	Military

SPRING

SPRING

1 | ALFRED THE GREAT

S ome nations rename their high streets and airports when their dead heroes are still warm. Others use the epithet 'great' to describe every statesman they produce who stays the right side of the law, and some who don't.

For the English, it is the other way around. Only one king of England was ever called 'the Great' and he was born and died so long ago that it is hard to verify whether he was great or not. We don't even know where his bones lie, though they were scattered by Puritans during the Eighteenth Century, so perhaps that is forgivable.

It is strange that we know so little about Alfred the Great. Perhaps the only inhabitants of England who are constantly reminded of him are those who live in his former capital city of Winchester, where a prominent statue of the man, wielding a sword, dominates the entrance to the city from the south.

Traditionally, what everyone knew about Alfred was the story of the cakes. This was a tale told by an anonymous monk writing the life of Alfred's advisor St Neot. It explained how the king, cornered by the Vikings at Athelney, goes wandering among his people deep in thought, knocks on a swineherd's hut and agrees to mind the stove for the wife. He was so deep in thought that he let the cakes burn, and received a heavy tongue-lashing – even perhaps a beating – without revealing who he was.

Now this story is pretty much forgotten, yet it has something in common with many English tales. It isn't really about the humiliation

3

of the king, or his dutiful acceptance of chastisement. It is about the ability of an ordinary housewife to upbraid the monarch. It is about the importance of practicality over intellect – a very English idea – and also about the importance of trying again. Alfred was soundly beaten by the Danes when he was hiding in Athelney, but he was thinking about how to have another bash at them. Alfred and the Cakes is the English equivalent of Robert the Bruce and the Spider: it is a story designed to encourage you never to give up.

The fact that Alfred didn't give up was partly what made him great. There he was, encircled with his followers on the Isle of Athelney, poking out over the waterline in the Somerset Levels, and yet he managed to gather an army, harry the Vikings and eventually defeat them – forcing his opponent Guthrum to become a Christian as part of the peace settlement.

Alfred was born in 849 in Wantage, into a world that was under threat. The Viking raiders had emerged from the sea to attack the monastic island of Lindisfarne in 793, and from there they went on to take over most of what we now know as England. Like Winston Churchill, Alfred inherited power at the moment of complete disaster, in 870 – but fought his way back to strength.

The Victorians loved Alfred as the symbol of the Anglo-Saxon race, which they believed was the basis of English greatness, for his wisdom and his books and translations, for founding the English navy and for building the first wharves that turned London into a port. They worshipped the Anglo-Saxons even though they had been pushed aside by a ruling class descended from Norsemen, or 'Normans' as they were called by then.

Yet they loved Alfred also for overcoming adversity – not just the Vikings but continual ill health. There is some evidence that he suffered from Crohn's disease.

Yet, even before the Victorian middle classes got hold of his memory, Alfred was a symbol for radical generations before, as the author of what they called the Laws and Liberties of Old England, which had been bundled away into history by William the Conqueror. In fact, Alfred's laws are a little vague, about keeping oaths and promises – and being able to write in English if you wanted to be a judge. Important in their own way, but not exactly Magna Carta.

Ironically, given how little has been preserved in writing from this time, Alfred's son insisted that it was important that laws should be written down so that they should not be 'brought to naught by the assault of misty oblivion'; a fate Alfred himself has so far managed to avoid, but only just.

Remember what punishments befell us in this world when we ourselves did not cherish learning nor transmit it to other men.

Alfred the Great

2 | ALLOTMENTS

The allotment movement has become an increasingly popular part of life in England, and a political ideal that began with the Agricultural Labourers' Strike of 1878. The idea of a small patch of land for the landless stretches back directly to the medieval commons, where ordinary people could use land to graze a cow or provide themselves with basic necessities. It certainly didn't begin that day of the great farmworkers' rally in Leamington during the strike, but the demonstration launched the political career of one campaigner in particular who was to make the allotments ideal central to his political life.

It is nearly a century and a half since Jesse Collings began his bid for 'three acres and a cow' for anyone who wanted them. Even at the time, when the campaign reached its height in the 1880s, it seemed politically impossible to provide that amount of land to everyone. His work culminated in the 1908 Allotments and Smallholdings Act, which – for peculiar reasons – Collings actually opposed, and which gave local councils a duty to provide allotments to anyone wanting one.

There have been bursts of enthusiasm for similar ideas in the century that followed – perhaps not for acres and cows, but for a small strip of land to grow vegetables, to feed the family or to get closer to nature. But now the demand is suddenly unquenchable. There are thought to be about 6 million people interested in having an allotment, with waiting lists as long as forty years in one London borough. It isn't quite clear why this change of heart occurred, but it may be that the real question is why their popularity ever went away, given the success of the Dig for Victory campaign in the Second World War.

Going Back to the Land was promoted between the wars by right-wing romantic groups like English Mistery and English Array, and by Oswald Mosley's British Union of Fascists. Mosley's enthusiastic acolyte, the novelist Henry Williamson, took it so seriously that he bought a farm in Norfolk and struggled with farming it throughout the war. His agricultural advisor Jorian Jenks – later one of the founders of the Soil Association – urged that Britain should grow all its own food, with fixed prices, low-rate loans for farmers, small-scale farming, and so on.

These were exactly the policies brought in by the agriculture minister Sir Reginald Dorman-Smith in 1939. Dorman-Smith was a former member of English Mistery, with its opposition to tinned food and the degradation of the soil, and also the architect of Dig for Victory.

Dig for Victory changed everything. There were 1.4 million allotments by 1943, by which time over a million tonnes of vege-tables a year were being grown in gardens, parks and on wasteland. There were radio programmes (3.5 million people tuned in to C. H. Middleton's gardening slots), even Dig for Victory anthems. By 1970, only a generation after the end of the war, there were just 530,000 allotments left, and a fifth of those were vacant. What went wrong?

Perhaps it was the end of rationing in 1954, and the beginning of self-service supermarkets (1950) which ushered in a new sense of plenty. Perhaps the remains of the sturdy working-class image of allot-ments made them seem old-fashioned. Policymakers had a housing crisis on their hands, and then a balance of payments crisis followed by an energy crisis.

Maybe that is what went wrong for the allotments movement in the 1950s. Official policy turned against romantic enthusiasm for growing things. Whatever happened, something has now shifted back: and we appear to be going through another period of the most English brand of radicalism of them all – the idea of going Back to the Land.

> I discovered at last, that even in all that labyrinth of the new London by night, there is an unvisited hour of almost utter stillness, before the creaking carts begin to come in from the market gardens, to remind us that there is still somewhere a countryside. And in that stillness, I have sometimes fancied I heard, tiny and infinitely far away, something like a faint voice hailing and the sound of horse hoofs that return.
>
> *William Cobbett*

3 | APOLOGIES

There's something in the English soul that believes apologies should always be reciprocated. It is important somehow not to be out-apologised, and it is quite possible for the English – especially the middle classes – to pre-empt apologies with agonising politeness when someone treads on their toes or runs into them in the street. Though, of course, they would be deeply offended if the person failed to apologise back.

Where does this delicacy come from? It isn't really that the English are any more tentative or nervous than other nations – quite the reverse. But they do hate confrontation, which the pre-emptive, polite apology is designed to avoid. And so the English grasp at opportunities to diffuse or avoid dangerous incidents which risk developing into unseemly fracas. This can give the impression to outsiders that the English are a formal nation. Actually, they can be a good deal less formal than their continental neighbours. It's just that they don't like the intimacy of a stand-up row. It is just so embarrassing.

Puritanism, along with the British stiff upper lip, which appears to have been invented by the Duke of Wellington, perhaps during the long summer evenings of the Peninsular Campaign, have won out over old English spontaneity. But this was not always the case. 'English girls are divinely pretty and they have one custom which cannot be too much admired,' wrote Erasmus on a visit to London at the end of the fifteenth century. 'When you go anywhere on a visit, the girls kiss you. They kiss you when you arrive. They kiss you when you go away. They kiss you when you return. Once you have tasted how soft and fragrant those lips are, you could spend your life there.' This is not a view of London that has been passed down through history.

An unfortunate side effect of the culture of the pre-emptive apology is that the English tend to suffer poor service or poor food in silence – not because they don't resent it (the English moan on with the best of them in the privacy of their own kitchens), but because they don't like to complain.

The great English comedienne Joyce Grenfell played the ultimate cringe-making complaint scene as the manager of a small guest house in Brighton, in the 1953 film *Genevieve*. Hot baths are to be procured only between two and four o'clock in the afternoon, she explains to her arriving guests. The room is decorated in brown and opens out on to a deafening chiming clock. When the young couple storm off, the manageress is mortified and turns to the other guests with English horror.

'No one's ever complained before,' she says.

One old lady stares up at the disappearing couple and asks: 'Are they Americans?'

How to apologise in English, according to Bloomsbury International English courses:

1. Sorry.
2. I'm so / very / extremely / terribly sorry.
3. How careless of me!
4. I shouldn't have . . .
5. It's all my fault.
6. Please don't be mad at me.

7. I hope you can forgive me / Please forgive me.
8. I cannot say / express how sorry I am.
9. I apologise for . . . / I'd like to apologise for . . .
10. Please accept my (sincere) apologies.

There is a strange paradox about the English global image: on the one hand it is about bucolic self-satisfaction and order ('There'll always be an England, while there's a country lane'); the English are seen to exude tradition and stuffy decorum; and are portrayed in foreign films as stiff idiots or as psychopaths seeking global domination. Yet look at England: there's an eighty per cent urban population and has been for a century. The English are forerunners in technology, from the Industrial Revolution to the Internet and are pre-eminent in advertising and youth culture.

When the Beatles emerged from Liverpool with their first hit record in 1962, they embodied this mismatch between the image and reality of England more than anything else, before or since. There was the prime minister, an Edwardian buffer called Harold Macmillan, the changing of the guard, the old men who – as the poet John Betjeman put it – 'never cheated, never doubted'. Then suddenly, there were these four young men with long hair, who took the hallowed American pop charts by storm, grasped the 1960s by the throat, dominating the psychedelic wave that followed and have been pasting their songs all over our memories ever since. They provided a backdrop to everyone's lives during the late twentieth century, and way beyond England.

The paradox goes deeper than that. John Lennon's middle name was Winston, though he later swapped it for something more appropriate. Paul McCartney's lyrics for 'When I'm Sixty-Four' may have shown a delicate understanding of the England of their parents' generation too – and the simple longing for 'a cottage in the Isle of Wight / If it's not too dear' – but it was McCartney who wrote it; Lennon explained that he would 'never write a song like that'.

The band began as the Quarrymen and managed to test out a number of other names – the Blackjacks and Johnny and the Moondogs – before they settled on the Beatles, and Lennon's friend and early band member Stuart Sutcliffe had his hair cut in the famous style on a trip to Hamburg with the band. They attracted the attention of local record-store owner Brian Epstein in 1962 and the recordings at Abbey Road Studio in London followed. By the autumn of 1963, hundreds of screaming fans greeted them at Heathrow Airport in the rain and Beatlemania had begun.

The Fab Four (a phrase coined by their press officer Tony Barrow) – John Lennon, Paul McCartney, George Harrison and Ringo Starr – hit the American market in 1964 and it was in the USA in the summer of that year that the folk singer Bob Dylan introduced them to cannabis (their dentist secretly added LSD to their coffee the following year). It was an important cross-cultural moment. By the time the band broke up, just six years later, they had become the most famous and successful rock group in history, selling around 600 million records.

Their cultural influence was immense, whether it was the creative flair of *Sgt. Pepper's Lonely Hearts Club Band* (1967) or any of their later work, but between them they seem to have laid the foundation of a fusion of English and American culture that still resonates.

Lennon was shot dead in New York in 1980 and Harrison died of cancer in 2001, though the two surviving members of the group continue to play their part in English life – McCartney playing at the Queen's Golden Jubilee concert and Starr narrating *Thomas the Tank Engine* – another seminal cultural export from the English north-west.

Beatles statistics:

Number of Beatles albums sold worldwide: 600m
Number of copies of *Sgt. Pepper's Lonely Hearts Club Band* sold in the UK: 4.5m
Number of No. 1 hits written by McCartney: 32
Number of Beatles' songs with a woman's name in the title: 18

I f many of the quintessentially English elements listed in this book actually came from somewhere else, the exception is beer. The link between England and beer goes back so far that it actually predates the English themselves, because it was being consumed in these islands for some centuries before the arrival of Hengist, Horsa, Cerdic or any of the other Anglo-Saxons.

The Celts certainly brewed ale from malt, water and yeast, and the Romans – having sent Caractacus off to Rome – carried on the same tradition. In fact, we even know the name of one Roman brewer. He was called Atrectus the Brewer and he came from Vindolanda on Hadrian's Wall, a place where surviving the winter probably required a great deal of beer-drinking.

Since this is one tradition that really does go right back, we are forced to conclude that the link between beer and these islands really is something to do with the climate. The key point is that the climate was not, except perhaps until recent years, very good for growing grapes, which ruled out making wine. What else was there to do, in fact, than make beer? The result: they made beer in the most enormous quantities, house by house, pub by pub, and river by river.

Strictly speaking, this wasn't actually beer but ale: by definition it could not be beer until hops were added, and – admittedly – this was not an English innovation. In fact, you can almost hear the squalls of protest when the first hopped beer was imported from the Netherlands in the fifteenth century. There was indeed opposition to the idea, but the only regulation was that brewers were not allowed to produce both beer and ale. It had to be one or the other.

Not only have they been at it for a long time, the English have also always drank a prodigious amount. By the late Middle Ages, this seems to have been an average of sixty to sixty-six gallons a year per head of population – men, women and children. Perhaps this was inevitable when beer was drunk at every meal and was practically the only safe liquid available.

That was one reason why, at the dawn of the Industrial Revolution, campaigners like William Cobbett were sharpening their pens at the expense of tea – sapping the moral strength of the nation – and urging people to go back to drinking beer.

One of the peculiar aspects of English life, well into the twentieth century, was the enormous quantity of beer that was drunk, especially after factory shifts – when anything up to fifteen pints might be drunk by an industrial worker escaping from the furnaces.

It was in the twentieth century that the traditional English warm beer (actually cellar temperature), and its variations – bitter, mild, brown, India pale, and all the other London specialities, drawn from casks on tap at the bar – began to make way for the array of refrigerated international lagers produced by multinationals.

The English never made a fuss of their beers. They had no beer festivals like the Americans. They had no Oktoberfests like the Germans. So they stood drinking by the bar without really noticing that their beer companies had been consolidated and consolidated until there was nothing left except global mush. Nor did they realise that much the same was happening to their pub chains.

One very important innovation for the English came in 1963 with the legalisation of home brewing. At last, it meant that anyone could make their own beer again. In fact, it is here that the English have been masterminding something of a fightback for their own culture – via the microbreweries and the brewpubs, where they have been once more brewing their own beer, and via the Campaign for Real Ale that has popularised the insurgency.

> The Rat, meanwhile, was busy examining the label on one of the beer-bottles. 'I perceive this to be Old Burton,' he remarked approvingly. 'Sensible Mole! The very thing! Now we shall be able to mull some ale. Get the things ready, Mole, while I draw the corks.'
>
> *Kenneth Grahame,* The Wind in the Willows *(1908)*

The peal of church bells along a string of different permutations and combinations, known as change ringing, is distinctively English. There are church bells in other countries too, of course, but the practice of ringing them was different in England, partly because the bells were bigger, the bell towers sturdier, and the bells were able to rotate through 180 degrees. It was partly also because of the involvement of seventeenth-century mathematicians – including Richard Duckworth and Fabian Stedman, whose book *Tintinnalogia* was published in 1668 – who rescued the whole business of bell-ringing from the Puritans by pointing out the complicated maths involved.

There have been bells all over Europe since the 1260s. They used to act as the local clock, tolling the hour when people should get up, start work, stop work and go to bed. There are still curfew bells tolled in at least three places around England, including Berwick-upon-Tweed. But it was the English who really took bells to their hearts. There are funeral bells and wedding bells and bells which sound for invasion, which is why bell-ringing was banned from 1940 to 1945. There are ghostly bells which toll from the sea, located offshore at Dunwich and Selsey. There is even a murder mystery about bell-ringing, in Dorothy L. Sayers' *The Nine Tailors* (1934).

England's robust bell towers also played a role in signalling danger, whether it was for seeing the beacons lit to warn people of the arrival of the Armada of 1588 or the complex system of semaphore, from church tower to church tower, which could carry a signal from the Admiralty in London to Nelson's fleet at anchor in Portsmouth Harbour in just twelve minutes.

The year 1668, when *Tintinnalogia* was published, also marked the birth of an otherwise ordinary and forgotten guardsman called John Hatfield. He was a sentry at Windsor Castle in 1690, or thereabouts, when he was court-martialled for falling asleep on sentry duty on the terrace. At his trial, he vehemently denied it, and to prove he had been awake at midnight – when he was accused of being asleep – he said he had heard something very strange. Far across the countryside of the Thames Valley, he had heard Great Tom – the bell in the tower opposite Westminster Hall – chiming thirteen times. Needless to say, this story did not go down well with the court. In fact, as far as they were concerned, it tended to prove his guilt. He was condemned to death.

Before the hanging could be carried out, over the next few days, the news of his claims reached Westminster. Several people swore that, on the night in question, they had also heard Great Tom strike thirteen. It was a peculiarity of the mechanism caused by the lifting piece holding on too long. It seemed highly unlikely that Hatfield could have heard it as far away as Windsor, but the fact that he did proved his innocence. William III pardoned him. History does not relate what happened to him later, but he died at his home in Glasshouse Yard, Aldersgate, on 18 June 1770, well into the reign of George III, at the age of 102.

Great Tom was an ancient thirteenth-century bell, which used to be known as Edward, until the Reformation. The bell tower was demolished in 1698 and the bell sold to St Paul's Cathedral. On the way there, it fell off its wagon at Temple Bar and cracked, was left in a shed in the cathedral for some years and was eventually recast in 1709 – in the Whitechapel Bell Foundry which still exists – and hung in the bell tower of St Paul's where it sounds the hour to this day.

It is also used to toll for the deaths of members of the royal family, the Bishop of London, the cathedral's dean and the lord mayor – if he dies in office – but that, as Rudyard Kipling might say, is another story.

King Edward III made and named me
So that by the grace of St Edward the hours may be marked

Translation of the Latin inscription inside the Great Tom bell

There is no more distinctive or iconic English building than the peculiar neo-Gothic clock tower that marks the boundary between the Palace of Westminster and Westminster Bridge. The tower itself looks too modern and compact somehow to be medieval, yet it soars like a cathedral above the clock face – the climax of so many films, from *The Thirty-Nine Steps* to *Thunderball*. It is instantly recognisable and not very pretty.

This is not the view of Augustus Pugin, the pioneer of neo-Gothic, for whom the clock tower was his last great achievement, and one which drove him to exhaustion and insanity.

The Clock Tower, as it has been called since then, was recently renamed the Elizabeth Tower after the Queen in honour of her Diamond Jubilee in 2012, but it hasn't caught on. England is not, after all, a nation that often renames its streets and buildings in honour of the recently departed or the living.

As everyone knows, Big Ben actually refers to the bell, which is now as familiar as the tower that houses it, because we hear it every day on the BBC before news bulletins. Its strange ding-dong-ding-dong chimes (said to have been adapted from Handel for the bells of Great St Mary's in Cambridge) are also familiar from television satire, annoying ringtones and much else besides.

When it was built, there was a row about the clock because nobody got round to commissioning one until the tower was 150 feet off the ground and it did not sit in its rightful place until 1859, twenty-five years after the old Palace of Westminster and parliamentary buildings had burned down.

The bell was already up by then, but not without difficulty. When Big Ben was being tested, it cracked in 1857 and had to be recast. It was hung in 1858, tested and cracked again in 1859, and remains cracked to this day. The solution was an English compromise: a lighter hammer. The bell finally tolled again in 1863. At 315 feet in height, and with no lift, it is a bit of a climb to see inside the careful mechanism and the Victorian pennies which still keep time – a penny is said to shift the timekeeping by 0.4 seconds a day one way or the other.

Big Ben is said to have been named after Benjamin Hall, the commissioner of the works. But there is an alternative story that Big Ben actually referred to Benjamin Caunt, a famous prizefighter, nicknamed by the workmen who had to heave the bell up and down, because of its weight.

As well as the cracks, another problem with Big Ben is that it is built on what used to be Thorney Island, on a sandy river beach connected to a marshy tract of land between two channels of the River Tyburn. The Victoria Tower at the other end – the tallest building in the country when it was built – was actually built on quicksand. When Westminster Underground station was enlarged, the huge tunnelling equipment had to stop work when Big Ben began to list. It now leans slightly to the north-west and oscillates very slightly according to the weather, rather like the MPs in the debating chamber below.

Big Ben is a kind of byword for English reliability, breaking down seriously only once in August 1976 – during the long hot summer that changed England forever, first bringing restaurant tables on to the London streets. It stopped again rather mysteriously, also in very hot weather, in May 2005.

It remains the icon of Englishness, understated, bizarrely antique-looking and thoroughly reliable, its pale moon face visible through the fogs and drizzle, its pilot light at the top indicating that Parliament is sitting, Members of Parliament are wrestling with the issues of the nation and all is right with the world.

> All through this hour
> Lord, be my guide
> And by Thy power
> No foot shall slide.

The lyrics of the chimes, as set out
on the wall of the Clock Tower

I n 1933, Winston Churchill's playboy son Randolph pulled a few strings and got his old housemate John Betjeman a job on the *Evening Standard* gossip column. It was then edited by the former spy Robert Bruce-Lockhart and, although Betjeman was no spy, he was rather a gossip.

Even so, he wasn't exactly equipped for the task. One of his first missions was to interview the Hollywood film star Myrna Loy, then at the height of her fame. Unsure what to ask her, Betjeman – the future Poet Laureate – quizzed her about the subject closest to his heart. 'Do you like perpendicular architecture?' he asked. He managed to persuade her to say that she was 'very interested'.

But then there is nothing more English than the perpendicular style. It is the English version of Gothic, and it has a particular tone – gentler perhaps than the Gothic which emerged from France at the abbey church of St Denis in 1144. Strictly speaking, it is the style of Gothic that emerged in the 1360s out of the horror of the Black Death, with its yearning, vertical lines, and its long, stretching windows.

This is the style exemplified in the soaring nave of Canterbury Cathedral, the creation of the most famous English architect of the medieval era, Henry Yevele. Of all the examples of perpendicular, Canterbury Cathedral is perhaps the best known, with its tower and flying buttresses added over the following centuries (one tower wasn't built until 1858).

Canterbury is English in other ways. Like so much of English history, the very stones of Canterbury Cathedral echo with a bloody history, as well as a spiritual one. Thomas Becket was murdered there, on the steps between the crypt and the choir, his brains flung around the stones by the end of a sword, by four knights who thought they were carrying out the enraged instructions of Henry II. Becket was actually the second of four archbishops of Canterbury to die violently in office (the first was Alphege, carried off by Vikings and done to death in Greenwich, in 1012).

The cathedral had something of a crisis in the 1170s. Becket was murdered at the end of 1170, and was soon canonised, so providing the cathedral with extraordinary wealth over the next three and a half centuries as a centre for pilgrimage, along the Pilgrims' Way from London and Winchester. In the mid-1170s the old cathedral choir caught fire and burned down, which meant major rebuilding. There had been churches on the spot way before the arrival of St Augustine in 597. There had been a Roman church on the same site and probably holy structures even earlier. It was only as of 1174 that the cathedral took on its new Gothic guise. The initial work was carried out by the French architect William of Sens, who first brought a hint of Gothic to these shores. But William fell from his own scaffolding and paralysed himself, naming William the Englishman as his successor.

This William extended the building eastwards for what became the Trinity Chapel, a repository for the remains of the newly canonised St Thomas Becket. Originally the new chapel just held the top of Becket's skull, sliced off by his assassins. After 1220, his tomb was moved there too. His feast day was also moved, from the end of December to the end of July, to make the progress less muddy for the pilgrims. After three more centuries of pilgrimages and miracles, by the reign of Henry VIII the tomb had a wooden cover which could be raised to reveal all kinds of precious stone.

This was something that a tyrannical king like Henry could never endure and he summoned Becket to be tried for treason. Having been dead for some centuries, Becket quite reasonably failed to appear and he was tried in his absence, found guilty and twenty-six carts arrived at the cathedral to confiscate his jewels.

An unmarked tomb was discovered in the crypt in 1888, to great excitement, and even as recently as 1990 two former Foreign Legionnaires were arrested in the cathedral in the middle of the night with a map drawn by a French archaeologist and a crowbar, intending to open the tomb of Cardinal Châtillon (died 1571), believing that Becket's bones were in there instead.

It is a very English mystery, and more English than it seems at first sight. The nostalgic belief in a continuing link from our own Protestant age to the old English Catholic faith – and a continuing symbol of resistance to the power of the state – is not just romantic, it is also tremendously English.

In the meantime, the archbishops of Canterbury continue to sit, with their palace at Lambeth, as knitted into the state as it is possible to be – second in precedence only to the monarch. There have been 105 of them as I write, all boasting the peculiar, slightly simian title 'Primate of all England'.

The four martyred archbishops:

Alphege (murdered by captors, 1012)
Thomas Becket (murdered by assassins, 1170)
Thomas Cranmer (burned, 1556)
William Laud (beheaded, 1645)

When Christopher Columbus stormed around the Caribbean, one of the reasons that he remained convinced, until his dying day, he had discovered a westerly route to China was that the so-called Indians he found on Cuba were wearing cotton shirts. They must have come from the East, from where all cotton came.

The English were late into the exploring game; John and Sebastian Cabot, who provided the basis for the original English claim to America, were from Venice and Genoa, and escaping from debtors when they arrived in Bristol and persuaded a parsimonious Henry VII to give them a contract to seek out lands 'unknown to all Christians'. Cotton was hardly on any English wishlists at that stage. The cotton trade was dominated by Antwerp and Venice.

The origins of growing cotton are lost in the mists of time. It certainly took place at least 7,000 years ago in Peru and Mexico in the West and in India in the East. The soldiers of Alexander the Great began wearing cotton once his armies reached India in 326 BC. So how did the story of cotton as a global commodity become entwined with that of the English? The answer is the success of the East India Company, which began importing it in great quantities in the middle of the seventeenth century.

By then, the English had become bored by wool, which had previously underpinned their wealth. It was too heavy, too unyielding, too English. As a result, in the eighteenth century, cotton became increasingly coveted, imported from India in those East Indiaman ships, with their red striped flags. It was light and easy to wash and you could print patterns on it. No wonder the fashionable sets loved it.

The key dates in the story of cotton in England are 1764 when James Hargreaves invented the spinning jenny in Lancashire, and 1771 when Richard Arkwright opened his mill in Derbyshire. From then on, cotton powered the Industrial Revolution in England as surely as coal and steam. Along the great rivers of the Midlands and the north, Blake's satanic mills puffed and panted as men, women and children struggled with the looms to turn the imported cotton from India and America into cotton goods for export to the world. By the time Nelson sighted the Franco-Spanish fleet at Trafalgar, more than forty per cent of English exports were made of cotton.

At that time, the main source of cotton was from the Deep South of the USA, where it was produced by slaves. This is both the dark stain on England's history, and its opposite. Yes, they traded the slaves who produced the cotton, financed by English bankers, reworked in English mills by children doing twelve-hour days in appalling heat. And yet it was England itself that abolished the slave trade and eventually vowed to stamp out slavery from the globe, and – very slowly – began to see that the economics of their factory labour was in itself a kind of slavery too.

In fact, so dependent were they on American cotton imported from the blockaded South during the American Civil War that Britain came very close to entering the war on the side of the slave-owners of the South. It was an irony for the nation which was still congratulating itself for abolishing slavery in its empire.

Another cruel irony was that India, which had first clothed Alexander's troops, and sold cotton clothing to Vasco da Gama, was soon importing cotton products from factories in Lancashire.

The English textile industry was hit hard by the American Civil War and the Union blockade. It was hit hard again by Gandhi's boycott of English cotton goods. It was hit again as the remaining clothes retailers increasingly began to outsource their production in the twentieth century. Marks & Spencer, the clothes retailer founded by a Jewish émigré from what is now Poland, was selling one in four pairs of cotton socks in the UK by 1930. It then formed a series of strategic partnerships with textile companies, starting with Corah in Leicester. The partnerships lasted for most of the rest of the century but, by the 1990s, there were only ten big English and Scottish clothing manufacturers left, supplying two thirds of M&S clothing. But they were being squeezed hard by the company, just as food suppliers would later be squeezed so hard by the big four supermarkets. Corah, the start of Marks & Spencer's quest for long-term relationships, was among those which were now in trouble and losing money. It was taken over by a finance company Charterhall in 1989 and then broken up.

By the end of the century, the other suppliers had all gone. It was the end of the close English relationship with cotton. Not really a happy story after all.

Without the firing of a gun, without drawing a sword, should they make war upon us, we could bring the whole world to our feet. What would happen if no cotton was furnished for three years? . . . England would topple headlong and carry the whole civilized world with her. No, you dare not make war on cotton! No power on earth dares make war upon it. Cotton is king.

Speech to the US Senate on why the north of the USA would never make war on the South, Henry Hammond, 1858

I f William Wordsworth is the most famous English poet, then his 'I wandered lonely as a cloud' must be our most famous poem – and he comes face to face in it, as everyone knows, with a 'host of golden daffodils'. The poem was written around 1804 (the same year that Blake wrote 'Jerusalem') but refers to a specific incident, on a walk with his sister Dorothy, which has a date attached: 15 April 1802.

It is no coincidence that this was an April poem, because the daffodil has always been the most exciting and most unexpected herald of spring. It is of course the national flower of Wales, but also has special significance for the English as demonstrated by the sheer diversity of its names.

It is known as daffydowndilly, or the east lily, or fairy bells. It is was known as goose-flop in Somerset, as Lent pitcher in Devon, as Queen Anne's flower in Norfolk, as churn in Lancashire, as well as other West Country variants like cuckoo-rise or cowslip.

As for the poem, it was published in Wordsworth's 1807 collection, which was roundly condemned as puerile by Lord Byron. Even Wordsworth's great friend and fellow pioneer of Romantic poetry, Samuel Taylor Coleridge, called it mental bombast. But the English feel otherwise. All that contemporary contempt has not prevented it from becoming one of the nation's best-loved poems.

There is also something rather wonderful about daffodils themselves, and not just for their visual cheerfulness. It's a little-known fact that they are traditionally used as an emetic to create vomiting – they're mildly poisonous – and these days are a key ingredient in the drug to combat Alzheimer's disease.

When we were in the woods beyond Gowbarrow park we saw a few daffodils close to the water side, we fancied that the lake had floated the seed ashore & that the little colony had so sprung up – But as we went along there were more & yet more & at last under the boughs of the trees, we saw that there was a long belt of them along the shore, about the breadth of a country turnpike road. I never saw daffodils so beautiful they grew among the mossy stones about & about them, some rested their heads upon these stones as on a pillow for weariness & the rest tossed and reeled and danced & seemed as if they verily laughed with the wind that blew upon them over the Lake, they looked so gay ever dancing ever changing.

Dorothy Wordsworth's journal, 15 April 1802

There is an unexpected side of the English which can tolerate absolute disorder, as long as they can win. It is true of all those wild, courageous and hare-brained schemes devised by young officers in successive world wars. It is certainly true when England play football. It is also true in their peculiar enjoyment of financial hubbub.

So cast your mind back to the heyday of the East India Company, in the 1690s, when London's coffee houses became the chaotic centre of news, gossip and financial speculation. After the end of the Licensing Act in 1695, coffee houses began publishing newspapers themselves, just as the newspaper proprietors began to set up a rival chain of coffee houses. The result was the cacophony of gin, and riotous wheeler-dealing, as portrayed in contemporary prints.

Into this maelstrom strode a particularly English type, the semi-corrupt financial buccaneer. The model in this case was Sir Josiah Child, the former brewer from Portsmouth, who arrived in the financial markets, his baronetcy purchased, his pockets filled with nuggets of information, financial and otherwise, for dispensing where useful, to propel himself into a position of unparalleled corporate and financial power.

This is how the pamphleteer Daniel Defoe described his activities:

Does Sir Josiah sell or buy? If Sir Josiah had a mind to buy, the first thing he did was to commission his brokers to look sower, shake their heads, suggest bad news from India; and at the bottom it followed, 'I have commission from Sir Josiah to sell out whatever I can', and perhaps they would actually sell ten, perhaps twenty thousand pound . . . and initiated the crowd of jobbers into that dexterity on tricking and cheating one another, which to this day they are the greatest proficients in that this part of the world ever saw.

Child famously managed to bribe James II with £10,000, and used his influence to turn the East India Company into a financial and military powerhouse. No more would the company be the timid supplicant to eastern potentates, and monopolistic Dutch and Portuguese trading empires. 'John Company' would arm itself and found its own empire in India, and defend it with force of arms. To do that, it would need full monopoly powers, which is where bribery came in.

The East India Company has a central place in the history of the corporation, and in English financial history, with its striped red and white flag – probably the original of the Stars and Stripes. It had begun in a joint venture by London merchants, given the blessing of Elizabeth I in 1599 and called the Company of Merchant Venturers Trading with the East Indies.

It was the East Indies and not India where they were bound, because England was still at war with Portugal and Spain and the English ships would have to circumnavigate India without landing there. And so it was that a small fleet of six ships set sail in 1601, led by the 600-ton *Red Dragon*, bound for the spice islands.

The commander, James Lancaster, carried with him six letters from the Queen, with the names left blank, for the names of the foreign potentates to be filled in. They were greeted in Sumatra eighteen months later by the local ruler, who had heard recently about the defeat of the Spanish Armada and was anxious to acquaint himself with Englishmen. When they arrived back in London, there was a new king on the throne, Lancaster was knighted, and the East India Company was established.

The company went on to rule more of the populous nations of India and beyond, with a large private army to collect taxes. The two greatest employees of the company, Clive of India and Warren Hastings, had to account for their actions to Parliament back in London, but it didn't stop the company from growing more and more powerful. At the height of the company's 274 years in business, it controlled nearly half of world trade, employing some of the most fertile minds of the Georgian and Victorian ages as well – including John Stuart Mill, Thomas Love Peacock and Robert Malthus. It was probably the first global corporation that ever seemed too big to fail.

But it did fail in 1858, following the trauma of the Indian Mutiny, and its assets were nationalised to the British Crown, handing India and much of the East to the British Empire. It is now a byword for greed, imperialism, and the kind of slavery which comes from taxing people who have no income. But it is other things too: a romantic dream of the East and some explanation for the strange English yearning for the Orient.

There was always something magic, queer, unaccountable about it [the East India Company]. Clive knew perhaps what it was, but he died mysteriously and never said what he knew. The facts can always be collected. The ledgers and Minute books are all extant and can be read. Great modern cities, Calcutta, Bombay, even Delhi, can be visited. The evidences of the company lie scattered about Europe and Asia. Yet one has an odd feeling that the Company was not exactly that, and that the attempt to make the East mercantile on the European model ended by altering Europe and leaving the East, under the surface, untouched.

R. H. Mottram (1883–1971), novelist and former mayor of Norwich

Occasionally in the course of 1903, the year of the birth of Typhoo Tea, the *Daily Mirror* and the Suffragettes, a small group of friends and churchmen began meeting at the vicarage of St Mary's, in Primrose Hill in London, to talk about the terrible state of English hymns. It was hardly surprising that, after several discussions, they had decided to launch a new hymn book for the Church of England.

They were led by Canon Percy Dearmer, a vicar and committed Christian socialist who – in the great division inside the Anglican Church – was definitely on the 'high' side, committed to ritual rather than too much sermonising. The problem for Dearmer and his friends was that the only thing they liked about the existing market leader in hymn books, *Hymns Ancient and Modern*, was its deep maroon covers, in an era when most Bibles, prayer books and hymn books were implacably black. They didn't like its sentimentality or its Victorian air of judgement, and they disliked the implication that hymns were somehow an extension of the sermon, rather than part of the liturgy. It was time for something new.

The result was *The English Hymnal* – so English that the covers were green – which has been the mainstay of Anglicanism ever since. Dearmer included Blake's controversial hymn 'To Mercy, Pity, Peace and Love' after much argument within the group, as well as his own hymn – the mainstay of English primary education – 'Jesus Good Above All Other'. He also divided the hymns up according to the major events of the Christian year – a vital element of high Anglicanism – and by doing so, contributed to the almighty row that ensued when it was published on Ascension Day 1906. The Archbishop of Canterbury, Randall Davidson, even expressed the hope that it would never be used.

But it was, and one of the main reasons was the music. Ignoring the qualms of his friends about including Blake, Dearmer drew on the considerable skills of a well-known agnostic to take charge of the music. Ralph Vaughan Williams, later the much-loved composer of England's favourite piece of classical music, 'The Lark Ascending', made *The English Hymnal* a labour of love. He was famous for his pioneering collection of folk music – in fact, the headquarters of the English Folk Song Society is still just around the corner from Dearmer's parish church – and carefully wove together some of the best English hymns with some of the best traditional English music.

'I heard the voice of Jesus say' was set to the folk tune called 'Kingsfold'. There was new music too: Christina Rossetti's 'In the Bleak Midwinter', with music specially commissioned from Gustav Holst, was sung for the first time in Primrose Hill at Christmas 1905.

Dearmer included new hymns from people active in social issues, like Canon Henry Scott Holland's 'Judge Eternal Throned in Splendour' and G. K. Chesterton's 'God of Earth and Altar'. He cut out some of the objectionable lines and verses, including 'The rich man at his castle' from 'All Things Bright and Beautiful'.

His objective had been to make his hymn book absolutely universal, and he succeeded. You can still find copies of it all over the world, from Palestine to every corner of the African continent, one of the most enduring legacies of the empire On Which the Sun Never Set – partly a legacy of that very empire, of course. But Dearmer was being a little disingenuous: he also had an agenda. It was hardly surprising that the archbishop was upset – Dearmer wanted the church to have more ritual and liturgy, and to spread the use of the hymns as widely as possible – not as adjuncts to sermons, but as part of the changing seasons and the changing shape of the services. Not everyone approved.

'I think, at last, the people are beginning to join in that hymn,' one of Dearmer's curates told the organist at one stage.

'Oh! Then I'll change it,' he said, nervous of the congregation spoiling the perfect music. It was a frustrating business, but there is no doubt that Dearmer won his battle. *The English Hymnal* is now part of the furniture of England, and the English psyche. The culture is stiff with the phrases from his hymns, from 'When I Survey the Wondrous Cross' to 'Christ is Made the Sure Foundation'. We know the words, even if we have never been inside a church in our lives.

> And all must love the human form,
> In heathen, Turk, or Jew;
> Where Mercy, Love, and Pity dwell,
> There God is dwelling too.

> *The controversial verse of William Blake's hymn*
> *'To Mercy, Pity, Peace and Love' which divided the*
> *progenitors of* The English Hymnal

They say that good fences make good neighbours, so the English Channel has made good neighbours of the French and the English. But since the nations emerged, the two of them have managed to continue a healthy rivalry, however close they might be geographically or politically.

It works both ways: the English make fun of French emotional logic; the French make fun of English food and stuffy English pomposity. Sometimes this rivalry reaches some worrying extremes. Sometime during the Napoleonic Wars, it isn't quite clear when, except that the fear of a French invasion was running high, a French warship was wrecked off the beach of Hartlepool in a storm. The sole survivor who struggled ashore turned out to be a monkey, dressed as a Napoleonic sailor. The locals, convinced that this was what the mythical French looked like, hanged the money from the mast of its own wreck. Or so it is said.

There are a number of peculiar things about this story. One is that, if the locals really thought this was what the French looked like, then it may say more about Hartlepool than it does about English attitudes towards their Gallic neighbours. The other is that, if it happened at all, there have been suggestions that this was not actually a monkey at all, but a 'powder monkey', in other words, a boy. That would make the monkey incident a war crime.

Even so, the people of Hartlepool seem oblivious to this kind of darkness, and celebrate the incident by calling themselves the 'monkey-hangers'. The local football team Hartlepool United has a mascot called H'Angus the Monkey, and the goalkeeper used to hang it from the goalmouth in key matches. When a local student called Stuart Drummond stood for election as the town's mayor dressed as H'Angus in 2002, he was elected (and was re-elected twice more).

The reason this rather unpleasant story continues to have resonance is that Francophobia, or a mild dislike – or at least rivalry – with the French is part of the heritage of the English. They are hardly the only nation to share this trait – even the Americans had a burst of dislike for the French in the run-up to the Iraq War – but the English revel in it. Is it because of their differences?

Well, yes and no. Yes, the phlegmatic English, with their drizzle and execrable food, are certainly different from those excitable French. But no, the French language was partly incorporated into English thanks to the Norman invasion in 1066. Also, as well as putting up with countless English invasions during the medieval period – and a continuing English fascination for battles like Crècy, Agincourt and the Nile – there have been two moments in history (1421 and 1940) when England and France came within a whisker of merger. That was Winston Churchill's proposal after the fall of Paris to the Nazis.

The rivalry is also tempered by our huge admiration of the French, for their bistros and for their patisseries, and the smells of authentic shopping in every small village – for the smell of baking bread and sweat – and for their relaxed attitudes to extramarital affairs.

Somehow the exasperation of the French and English became embodied in the person of President Charles de Gaulle, who was a rather unwelcome, and slightly humourless, arrival in London in June 1940, and who still managed to veto British membership of the European Economic Community (as it was then) in 1963 and 1967.

There is a story told in Westminster of de Gaulle's state visit to

England in 1960, when at a formal dinner in the House of Lords the French president looked up during his meal to find himself staring at a huge painting of the Battle of Waterloo. It is said that he grabbed his plate and stormed round to the other side of the table, only to look up again and find himself staring at an enormous painting of the Battle of Trafalgar.

That story tells you everything you need to know about Francophobia. It is more a sensitivity and rivalry between allies – and the French have been English allies now since the Crimean War – than it is outright hatred. It is less blind dislike and more grudging *entente cordiale*, the 1904 side effect of Edward VII's love of the fleshpots of Paris.

But still the English can shake their heads at extraordinary examples of French sensitivity, and the French can shake their heads in despair and remind themselves of the boneheaded English headline: FOG IN CHANNEL – CONTINENT CUT OFF.

> In former times, when war and strife
> The French invasion threaten'd life
> An' all was armed to the knife
> The fishermen hung the monkey O!
> The fishermen with courage high,
> Seized on the monkey for a French spy;
> 'Hang him!' says one; 'he's to die'
> They did and they hung the monkey Oh!
> They tried every means to make him speak
> And tortured the monkey till loud he did speak;
> Says yen 'that's French' says another 'it's Greek'
> For the fishermen had got drunky Oh!

> *Ned Corvan, the Tyneside music-hall artist, c.1850*

14 | FULL ENGLISH

The term 'the full Monty' has become somewhat ambiguous. One of its many meanings is a 'full English', which means in effect a full English breakfast – the only recognisably, unambiguously English contribution to international cuisine.

There is something comfortably luxurious about a full English breakfast, in its complete failure to compromise with the modern standards for healthy eating or efficient throughput of guests through a given dining room. It takes ages to cook, takes ages to eat and takes months off your life with every bite, thanks to the lashings of cholesterol. It is boneheadedly, determinedly what it is – which is, let's not beat around the bush, fried eggs, fried bread, fried mushrooms, baked beans, fried tomatoes, sausages and great wedges of bacon.

Depending on where you are, those wedges of bacon may have shrunk somewhat as the water evaporates. There may also be a snippet of black pudding. There may be hash browns, though there is some controversy about the hash browns, which are strictly speaking an American addition.

There is some evidence that combining these elements into one extravagant dish goes back as far as the eighteenth century, which is pushing it since modern industrial bacon was hardly developed until then (in Wiltshire, or so they claim). Before that, English breakfasts normally involved bread, meat and ale. Even in the nineteenth century, Mrs Beeton was including additions like chops and potted fish in the mix. Parson James Woodforde, who wrote more about what he ate than about the religious services he presumably presided over, barely mentions what he consumed for breakfast.

By the twentieth century, you keep tripping over the full English. The great Edwardian house parties for the gentry and ruling classes were leisurely affairs where guests would drift down in the morning and help themselves from silver pots which were keeping the various elements of breakfast hot. Half a century later, the full English was a pretty classless affair. Every working man by the 1950s aspired to egg and sausage in the morning, come rain or shine.

It has even been suggested that its heyday was as recently as the 1960s, when every bed-and-breakfast outfit south of the Scottish border began offering the full English as its standard fare.

It may not be quite as good for you as a ubiquitous continental breakfast – which these days involves little more than an efficient croissant, coffee and yoghurt – but you certainly know afterwards that you have had breakfast.

Mrs Beeton's full English breakfast:

The following list of hot dishes may perhaps assist our readers in knowing what to provide for the comfortable meal called breakfast. Broiled fish, such as mackerel, whiting, herrings, dried haddocks, &c.; mutton chops and rump-steaks, broiled sheep's kidneys, kidneys à la maître d'hôtel, sausages, plain rashers of bacon, bacon and poached eggs, ham and poached eggs, omelets, plain boiled eggs, oeufs-au-plat, poached eggs on toast, muffins, toast, marmalade, butter, &c. &c . . .

Full English breakfast, as recorded bt Mrs Beeton in
The Book of Household Management *(1861)*

My aspens dear, whose airy cages quelled,
Quelled or quenched in leaves the leaping sun,
All felled, felled, are all felled;
Of a fresh and following folded rank
Not spared, not one

So said the English poet Gerard Manley Hopkins in 1879 when they felled the Binsey poplar trees along the side of Port Meadow outside Oxford. Still there beside the site of the poplars are the hedges and line of trees that marked the ancient boundary between Oxfordshire and Berkshire (the boundary is not there any more, since they reorganised such things in 1974). Hedges are celebrated, quite rightly, for their own sake as an environmental resource – though we have lost half of them since 1950 – but it is their role as boundary markers that make them especially important to the English psyche.

Boundaries are important to private people like the English, which is why English suburbs – a kind of reflection of at least one English state of mind – emphasise them as much as they do. In fact, boundaries are so important that, in ancient days, the children of the town were beaten at key points on the borders so that they remembered them – a ceremony known as beating the bounds, and which combined two of the less attractive English vices: an obsession with borders and a predeliction for corporal punishment.

Hedges are there as the remains of woods, or to provide a tall covering for the Saxon roads which, as G. K. Chesterton put it, were built by the 'rolling English drunkard'. They are there still to provide a crop of fruit for the villagers around the common land and the field strips, or (at least in Kent) to protect the hops from wind. These days they also provide a home for the birds and insects that are needed to seed the crops and support the basic underpinning that the natural world provides for all our lives. Of course, they also marked out the patterns of patchwork fields that tended to follow the enclosures of common land.

If you hurtled back to earth from space, the main clue you might find that you had landed in England are the hedgerows. They give an absolutely distinctive pattern to the countryside. If we never win a Test match again, wrote the poet Edmund Blunden in 1935, 'we shall still have the world's finest hedges'.

Quite so. The English are a nostalgic lot. Their very psyche is spaced out in hedgerows which divide their relationships and their lives. They feel emotional about hedges just as they feel devastated sometimes when their trees start disappearing in one of the increasingly common arborial epidemics. They wept over the elms in the 1970s, just as Hopkins wept over his aspens. They will weep again over the oak. Yet it is also part of the English character, for some reason, to do almost nothing about it.

Hedgerow plants:

Holly
Alder
Willow
Elm
Hazel

Maple
Buckthorn
Crab
Elder
Dogwood
Guilder rose
Privet
Wayfaring tree
Bramble
Tamarisk
Fuchsia
Dog rose
Burnet rose
Sweet rose
Sallow
Sloe
Blackthorn

I t is hard to entirely like Henry V in the Shakespeare plays that portray him either as king or as the calculating Prince Hal (in the two plays about his father), or even perhaps to like him much once he has become king and has slaughtered the nobility of France on the field of Agincourt. Perhaps anybody could be forgiven for a speech like 'the feast of Crispian' and other moments of heroism and charm which Shakespeare calls 'a little touch of Harry in the night'. But still, there seems to be a disturbingly calculating core to the man.

Despite Henry V's healing domestic policies, which involved restoring the exiles and being generally nice to people, he did a lot more than simply cut poor Sir John Falstaff on his coronation day ('I know thee not old man'). The original of Falstaff, the Lollard leader Sir John Oldcastle, was burned at the stake at the spot between London's Oxford Street and Tottenham Court Road now marked by a tower block called Centre Point. In fact, it was Oldcastle's public execution that is supposed to have cursed the spot so absolutely that the tower has never been fully tenanted, but don't let's be superstitious.

Clearly this reflects what Shakespeare felt. After all the sound and fury of Agincourt and victory over the French, and marriage to the beautiful Katherine of Valois, there is a brief epilogue explaining that Henry died young, handing the crown of France and England to his baby son 'whose state so many had the managing / That they lost France and made his England bleed'.

Henry certainly provided a glimpse of Arthurian glory for those who want it, but he was the Nearly Man of history – creating the conditions for one of those moments when France and England seemed set to merge (the other was 1940) but expiring of tuberculosis in a field in 1422. His intestines remained buried where he died and were recently uncovered in their original box. They still smelled bad.

His birth is a little obscure. Nobody recorded the date because he was never expected to be heir to the throne – let alone king – but he was always known as Henry of Monmouth and therefore had a good claim not to be English, but Welsh. In fact, as he says in Shakespeare's play, explaining how he occasionally wears a celebratory leek: 'For I am Welsh you know, good countryman.' Case closed.

But don't let's be curmudgeonly about Harry, or pour scorn on his strange pudding-basin haircut, or his poor luck in the annals of history. He still provides inspiration for English pluck and daring, especially when they are up against impossible odds – about double at Agincourt. And he inspired a great play.

When Laurence Olivier played Henry in his 1944 film, borrowing the Irish army as extras (they were paid more if they brought their own horse), he injected a splash of colour and excitement into English culture to coincide with D-Day, helped along by William Walton's classic score. Together they roused a war-torn nation, and ushered in a sense of colourful Englishness which carries on to this day.

And when all is said and done, there may be a little bit of some of us in England, now a-bed, who still 'think themselves accursed they were not here, / And hold their manhoods cheap, whiles any speaks / That fought with us upon Saint Crispin's day'.

I see you stand like greyhounds in the slips,
Straining upon the start. The game's afoot:
Follow your spirit; and, upon this charge
Cry 'God for Harry! England and Saint George!'

Henry V, sounding the charge at Harfleur

'Had we lived, I should have had a tale to tell of the hardihood, endurance, and courage of my companions which would have stirred the heart of every Englishman. These rough notes and our dead bodies must tell the tale, but surely, surely, a great rich country like ours will see that those who are dependent on us are properly provided for.'

That is the familiar final diary entry of Captain Robert Falcon Scott, found by his frozen body, written in a tent in an Antarctic blizzard. Somehow the words seem to sum up the English obsession with heroic failure. Roald Amundsen beat Scott to the South Pole; Ernest Shackleton succeeded in bringing all his men back from the Antarctic catastrophe alive. Yet it is Scott's failure to do either that somehow endeared him to the English.

The last sentence also reveals another English obsession: somehow holding together enough money to get by. It was Nelson's last wish for his family as well. And whilst some nations might shower their heroes and their loved ones with wealth, Nelson's partner Emma Hamilton died impoverished in her Calais lodgings in 1815.

Scott emphasised the point just before he died, in a final note written on 29 March 1912. Two weeks later, the luxury transatlantic liner *Titanic* hit an iceberg and sank with the loss of 2,224 passengers and crew: two of the greatest heroic failures in history, and just a few days apart.

But there are lighter sides to the English flair for heroic failure as seen in the case of Georgian actor Robert Coates, who used his fortune to finance plays in which he played major Shakespearean roles – especially Romeo – and brought the house down night after night with his disastrous performances.

During his first performance as Romeo, he got out his snuffbox on stage and offered some to the occupants of a box above him. During the death scene, he was careful to use his own hat as a pillow and a handkerchief to dust the stage where he was about to fall dead. On another occasion, he dropped a diamond buckle as he headed offstage and crawled around, interrupting the performance looking for it.

His performances were so funny that audience members were regularly treated for laughing too much. He was so impressed by the response to Romeo's death on one occasion that he repeated it, and would have done it again had not Juliet risen from the dead to stop him.

Coates was of English extraction, though he was actually born in the West Indies, and he was to die in a road accident outside the Theatre Royal, Drury Lane – but you can see something of the admiration of incompetence endures to this day. How else are we to explain the popularity of Eddie 'The Eagle' Edwards, the heroic English ski-jumper at the 1988 Winter Olympics?

Edwards continued in the same vein afterwards, releasing a record in Finnish, though he didn't actually speak the language. An example to us all.

Success is stumbling from failure to failure with no loss of enthusiasm.

Winston Churchill articulates the gentle English art of failing

I s it possible to pin down English humour and define it? It may only be possible to say that it appears to be part of the national character. This is not just what J. B. Priestley used to call 'humorous realism' – the ability to find very ordinary things and people funny, which goes back to Geoffrey Chaucer at least – but also the ability to find yourself rather funny too.

Which other nation could have poked so much fun at themselves during the 2012 Olympics opening ceremony? But then again, it was a British opening ceremony, where the artistic genius was actually Scottish. The English certainly take a particular enjoyment at their own peculiarities, even their own failures, that other countries lack almost completely. American office workers might struggle to publicly admit to 'an example of when they failed', but English counterparts remember their disasters as badges of honour.

This enjoyment of their own peculiarities seems to date back as long as the English have existed. 'I passed many hours with him on the 17th,' wrote James Boswell (a Scot) of Samuel Johnson, 'of which I find all my memorial is, "much laughing". It should seem he had that day been in a humour for jocularitie and merriment, and upon such occasions I never knew a man laugh more heartily.' Yet there was Boswell, not much later, describing his friend's 'perpetual gloom'. The two – humour and gloom – seem quite close companions, as perhaps they always are in great comedy, amongst the English.

Perhaps the clearest view of English humour is available by

comparing it more closely to American humour. English jokes in this respect seem to be based on exaggeration – they are whimsical, flights of fancy, imagining the world distorted, pushing those peculiarities to their logical conclusion. It is the exaggeration of an English joke that becomes, at some point, farcical nonsense: and from Lewis Carroll to Monty Python, the English have excelled at humorous nonsense (as opposed to serious nonsense in the Theatre of the Absurd, where the French clearly have the upper hand).

From Gilray to Giles cartoons, the root of English humour is exaggeration to the point of caricature. The way it is exaggerated may change – we don't find the humour of W. S. Gilbert, Dan Leno, Arthur Askey or *ITMA* funny in the way their our grandparents might have done – but that is just the nature of passing time. The basis remains the same, and the greatest English humorists – Jane Austen, Charles Dickens, P. G. Wodehouse, Stan Laurel or Charlie Chaplin – do still keep their ability to make people laugh, whether it is in the novel, the newspaper, the music hall or the comedy club, and there are certainly comedians to choose from in every generation.

This is what the great eighteenth-century essayist William Hazlitt said on the subject:

> The French cannot, however, be persuaded of the excellence of our comic stage, nor of the store we set by it. When they ask what amusements we have, it is plain they can never have heard of Mrs Jordan, nor King, nor Banniser, nor Suett, nor Munden, nor Lewis, nor little Simmons, nor Dodd, and Parsons, and Emergy and Miss Pope, and Miss Farren, and all those who even in my time have gladdened a nation and made life's business like a summer dream.

All these names who once strutted the boards of London are now forgotten, but their places are taken by others like them. There is perhaps a basic laziness about the English, an acceptance of life as it is, which makes us yearn for someone to make work feel like a summer dream – then we can forget ourselves for a moment, unbutton our buttoned-up coats, and just be a little less serious.

A woman gets on a bus with her baby. The bus driver says: 'Ugh, that's the ugliest baby I've ever seen!' The woman walks to the rear of the bus and sits down, fuming. She says to a man next to her: 'The driver just insulted me!' The man says: 'You go up there and tell him off. Go on, I'll hold your monkey for you.'

Voted funniest English joke in a poll of 36,000 people in 2010

Nationality gets to be a bit of a problem when it comes to King Arthur and his knights. If he existed, which he almost certainly did as the leader of the Romano-British kingdoms against the marauding Saxons, then he wasn't exactly English. Welsh, perhaps; Cornish, possibly. Roman, almost by default – his uncle was supposed to be the Roman general Ambrosius Aurelianus.

When it comes to his knights, the English claim on him becomes even more shaky. Sir Gawain definitely sounds Welsh. Sir Lancelot first appeared in French literature. Worse, the battles Arthur fought in recorded history – Wallop, Mount Badon – were almost certainly against the rampaging and still pagan English, not on their side at all.

This caused consternation among the authors of Edwardian boys' adventure stories, who were determined that heroes should be on the side of the Anglo-Saxons, but were also disconcerted that this meant he would have been fighting the Christians.

The first mention of King Arthur in any chronicle was in around 820, at least two centuries after his battles, and one of the candidates for the original Arthur – a king called Riothamus – was actually from Brittany.

What we can say about the great romantic tale of the British Isles, as the historian John Morris points out, is that 'Arthur' was suddenly and briefly a popular name for chieftains after this period, and that the great events probably took place on what is now English soil. Arthur's castle of Camelot may not have been 'many-towered', as Alfred Tennyson suggested, but the best-known site for it is South Cadbury, a vast windswept hill fort in Somerset. His round table – a medieval fake – is celebrated in Winchester, later the Anglo-Saxon capital of Wessex.

Then again, *Sir Gawain and the Green Knight* is one of the first stories in Middle English to survive. Gawain manages to resist cowardice and sexual temptation to keep his promised encounter with an axe-wielding green giant.

It was the Victorians who really took all that sacrificial chivalry of the Arthurian legends to their hearts, churning out great sombre poems (Tennyson, etc.) and even more sombre paintings (Burne-Jones, etc.), to encourage similar behaviour in the next generation.

Obediently, the Scott Antarctic expedition, and the upper-crust passengers on the *Titanic* – not to mention the officers at Mons and the Somme – went calmly to their deaths, thinking of Galahad, Tristram, Percival and all the others, vowing to be perfect knights.

HIC JACET ARTHURUS REX QUONDAM REXQUE FUTURUS
(Here lies Arthur, the king that was and the king that is to be)

Tomb inscription in Thomas Malory's Le Morte d'Arthur

Even more than the works of William Shakespeare, the translators of the Old and New testaments into English during the Reformation and pre-Reformation years left behind an extraordinary wealth of quotations, and a legacy of language which we all share in. Because of that, it is hard to imagine English without the great translation of the Bible ordered by the new king, James I, newly arrived from Scotland after the death of Elizabeth I.

The problem was that nobody could agree on a proper translation of the Bible in English. There were the translations of John Wycliffe and his friends, banned back in 1409. There was William Tyndale's version which formed the basis of Henry VIII's Great Bible, and the so-called Bishop's Bible designed to bring it all up to date – but it was vast and very expensive to get a copy. There was the Geneva Bible, translated by Protestants in exile during the reign of Queen Mary – known to history as Bloody Mary – which included a series of notes and comments which some people found offensive.

The problem for James and his churchman friends was that the people who had taken the trouble to translate the Bible into English had tended to be Protestants. And the translations showed a certain bias – the word 'congregations' rather than 'church' and other things that stuck in the Anglican gullet. What was needed was a translation that assumed the existence of bishops and ordained clergy.

Hence the conference at Hampton Court in 1604 which kickstarted the project. James had been mulling over the idea of a new translation of the Bible since 1601 when it was put forward as an idea by the Church of Scotland general assembly in Fife. Three years later, the translators were appointed, unpaid, to six translating committees in Oxford, Cambridge and Westminster to get the job done. In practice, the sheer beauty of Tyndale's version echoes still through the words of the new committee, with its starkness and simplicity.

Not everyone liked it. During the English Civil War a generation later, the Puritans had their own version of the Geneva Bible produced, and there were some important scholars who had been left out. Nobody would work with the greatest expert on Hebrew of the day, Hugh Broughton, so he didn't like it. In fact, he said that 'he would rather be torn in pieces by wild horses than that this abominable translation should ever be foisted upon the English people'.

But foisted it was, and all over the English-speaking world. The misprints and omissions of the early years – especially the notorious Wicked Bible of 1631 which left the word 'not' out of the adultery injunction in the Ten Commandments – were all put right in one definitive printed version in 1769.

Few people choose the King James version for everyday use these days. But for sheer poetry, you can't beat it.

In the beginning God created the Heauen, and the Earth. And the earth was without forme, and voyd, and darkenesse was vpon the face of the deepe: and the Spirit of God mooued vpon the face of the waters. And God said, Let there be light: and there was light. And God saw the light, that it was good: and God diuided the light from the darkenesse. And God called the light, Day, and the darkenesse he called Night: and the euening and the morning were the first day.

The beginning of Genesis Chapter 1, from the 1611 version

One of the most English of all the English eccentricities is the pursuit of bizarre archaeological theories and, the more they irritate mainstream historians, the better people seem to respond. Whole cults have grown up around the real identity of William Shakespeare, the fate of the princes in the Tower, the original rituals carried out at Stonehenge and much else besides. And who is to say they are wrong?

And so it was that businessman Alfred Watkins, an amateur archaeologist, was travelling in Hereford with his son – on 30 June 1921 to be precise – and looked up to see the ley lines criss-crossing the countryside, lit up like 'fairy lights'. He regarded them as notches on the hills to allow the Neolithic travellers to find their way from one place to another, as prehistoric trackways, dead straight. They seemed to stretch for miles and align ancient mounds or churches, and for no obvious reasons (one critic made the same case for telephone boxes).

It wasn't until 1969 that John Michell bundled the whole idea up with an English version of feng shui, plus geomancy and various other esoteric traditions, and shovelled them into his book *The View Over Atlantis*, and – at one stroke – founded the English tradition of earth mysteries. Soon writers like Iain Sinclair and Peter Ackroyd were exhuming myths of sacred geometry about the alignment of churches in London, the city founded, after all – according to Geoffrey of Monmouth – as the New Troy.

Mainstream archaeologists still resist the idea and there is little agreement what these alignments actually were – whether they were simple ways of finding your way across dense forest or whether they were some other kind of psychic mystery, or lines of force. Or the roads by which the dead left the world, or the paths by which witches flew. Or the outward manifestations of the energy flows of the earth itself.

Michell single-handedly added this kind of sacred English exoticism to the hippy and underground movement, popularising Glastonbury as the heart of the cult – transforming a rural backwater into an alternative mecca for the new movement. It was Michell who pointed out the existence of one of the longest ley lines of all, known now as the Michael Line, which stretches from Land's End in Cornwall all the way to Hopton-on-Sea on the Norfolk coast, in the direction of the rising sun on 8 May (St Michael's Day) or alternatively on May Day, depending on who you talk to.

It goes via a whole range of ancient sites, including St Michael's Mount and the church tower on the tip of Glastonbury Tor dedicated to, you guessed it, St Michael. But it wasn't for another fifteen years or so before the dowsers Hamish Miller and Paul Broadhurst took some dowsing rods and traced the line all the way, and found it really wasn't straight at all – and neither was the so-called Mary Line that intertwined it all the way (see *The Sun and the Serpent*, 1990).

Dowsing, incidentally, is the skill which usually allows people to sense the whereabouts of water. It is another esoteric – though highly practical – skill which is much used in England, and equally ignored by a sceptical mainstream, though it was declared illegal in 1572 because of supposed links to witchcraft. The fascination with the esoteric in English culture is accompanied by an instinctive fear of anything unusual in its bureaucracies and authorities.

The unconventional archaeologist Frederick Bligh Bond lost his job as director of excavations at Glastonbury Abbey when he started using automatic writing – receiving messages from a long-dead medieval monk – to guide his decisions about where to dig.

Still, whatever ley lines may or may not be, they provide an added layer of deep history – and maybe even deep mystery – which only underlines the sensible respectability of the National Trust or English Heritage. And they're enjoyable, if only for irritating the English academic establishment, who are no longer able to fall back on witchcraft legislation.

I knew nothing on June 30th last of what I now communicate, and had no theories. A visit to Blackwardine led me to note on the map a straight line starting from Croft Ambury, lying on parts of Croft Lane past the Broad, over hill points, through Blackwardine, over Risbury Camp, and through the high ground at Stretton Grandison, where I surmise a Roman station. I followed up the clue of sighting from hill top, unhampered by other theories, found it yielding astounding results in all districts, the straight lines to my amazement passing over and over again through the same class of objects, which I soon found to be (or to have been) practical sighting points.

Alfred Watkins, Early British Trackways (1922)

'Put your foot down, Tony. They're getting rather close,' says Camp Freddie in the passenger seat of a turbo-charged, strengthened Mini Cooper, dashing through the back streets of Turin with gold in the boot.

The Italian Job (1969) includes many of the trademark elements of English cinema in the 1960s: a crime caper where the rogues almost get away with it but not quite, where the humiliation for Johnny Foreigner is pretty complete, and where the diverse English classes rub along together upside down and inside out – the snobbish Mr Big of crime is in prison, and the action is led by a heroic cockney (Michael Caine).

The apotheosis of the Mini was undoubtedly this film, where red, white and blue Mini Coopers whizz through the Turin sewer system to escape from the Italian police. In fact, all three of the original Minis – which were supposed to be carrying more than one and a half times their own weight in gold in their boots – were written off in accidents in the sewers during filming.

By then the Mini, originally called the Austin Seven and the Morris Mini-Minor, was ten years old. As so often in iconic English style, it was designed by a man who wasn't English at all, but from the Greek community of Smyrna, whose grandfather had been awarded British citizenship after his work on the Smyrna–Aydin railway.

Sir Alec Issigonis was an instinctive designer. When one engineer asked him what size to make the wheels, he held his hands apart and said: 'This big.' The engineer measured his hands at ten inches and that was how big the wheels were.

Issigonis also designed the Morris Minor, which stayed in production between 1948 and 1971 as the quintessential preferred conveyance of the impoverished English middle classes. The Mini emerged from the energy crisis that followed the Suez Invasion of 1956, when Issigonis was asked by the British Motor Corporation to design a car which used less petrol.

It was launched in the summer of 1959 to an uncertain reception. This was just too new a concept, for people still used to running boards and strange indicator lights that stuck out of the side of the car. It wasn't until the Queen was photographed at the wheel of a Mini that the car began to gather to itself its extraordinary cachet. Soon there was hardly an English celebrity, whether it was David Niven or Peter Sellers, without one. The Beatles snapped up four of them.

The size of the Mini, which became such an iconic version of 1960s London, was achieved by mounting the engine sideways – a leap of imagination which had eluded car manufacturers before. That meant the car was only ten feet long, but could carry a whole family and their luggage. Over 5.3 million Minis came off the production line before it was finally stopped in October 2000, after an amazing forty-one years. In fact, it is quite impossible to imagine English life in the Elizabethan years, the second half of the twentieth century, without a Mini somewhere in the corner of the picture.

There was something of the era of miniskirts and instant mashed potato and instant coffee about the Mini – not just hassle-free, but compact, a pocket-sized car.

The right to use the name Mini was then taken over by BMW, but the new BMW Minis are not the same as the original designs, though even these bigger, sportier Minis – built at the BMW Cowley plant in Oxford – have been selling well. Whether they are quite Minis in the traditional mould remains a controversial subject.

> Just remember, in this country they drive on the wrong side of the road.
>
> *Charlie Croker in* The Italian Job

s it because of the use of sheds that the sports of pigeon-fancying and pigeon racing seem so English? Is it that peculiar link that working-class English males have to the wooden shack down the garden, full of nameless intricacies, that pigeon racing seems so much like a national sport? Or is it something to do with the squadrons of pigeons that used to descend on Trafalgar Square in London – until dealt with in one of the first acts of the new mayor of London in 2000?

That isn't clear. What is certain is that people have kept and bred pigeons in these islands, or used their homing instincts to deliver messages, for centuries and probably well into Roman times. But the sport of racing pigeons was actually developed by the Belgians, and it was only when the king of Belgium, the brutal Leopold II, gave the British royal family breeding birds that the sport began to take off over here in a big way. The first English pigeon race was held in 1881, encouraged mainly because the Belgians used to start their races from southern England.

Since then, the sport has been declining steadily – along with cloth caps and whippets – though it is attracting big money in the USA and so will almost inevitably be re-imported at some point. There remains something distinctively northern about pigeon-fancying, and there is the cliché of the clipped and reserved Yorkshireman who lavishes love and care on his pigeons, but finds it hard to do the same for his own children. It is a small slice of the great paradox of the English, for whom animals have often seemed a more comfortable conduit for love than human beings.

In fact, there is – as so often – rather a class divide involved. The working classes created their sheds out of old pieces of wood and scrap and concentrated on racing short distances, while the long-distance racers had to be aristocratic or anyway someone with the means to pay for it. The pigeons themselves came on to the market at low, affordable prices because the invention of the electric telegraph began to put them out of business as professional carriers of messages.

The return of pigeon post came during the siege of Paris in 1870–1; the English watched entranced as French pigeons carried over a million messages in and out of the city, over the Prussian lines. Then the rise of football as a working-class pastime in England in the final Victorian decades seems to have driven out the pigeons again. The days when the birds could be described as black caps, yellow boots and chockers, and the husky voices of a pigeon-fancier could be recognised immediately – maybe an early example of what we now know as pigeon-fancier's lung – have long gone.

But it has been a slow decline. The London, Midland and Scottish Railway reckoned it carried 7 million pigeons during the 1929 racing season. In 1934, one pigeon racer described his feelings when a fancier could see his own bird returning and stood 'transfixed, electrified; there comes the faint rustle of wings: almost simultaneously upon the small platform at the entrance to the loft, there is the bird of his dreams'. There is no doubt of the strange mixture of reticence and emotion about the whole thing.

For George Orwell, pigeon-fancying emphasised what he called the 'privateness' of English life. He even condemned as 'something ruthless and soulless' the health and safety housing improvement regulations, which attempted to stamp pigeons out.

He marched off with a bunch of flowers in his hand and several pigeon eggs in his overall pockets . . . On arrival home, he put the eggs in a basin on the sink, awkwardly, almost abruptly, he handed the flowers to mother. No words, no glances, just a muffled grunt that seemed to say all that needed saying.

William Woodruff describing his father's return to Blackburn from a pigeon race in The Road to Nab End *(2001)*

There is a certain kind of dull-headed English temperament that deeply disapproves of reading. It still exists, though people rarely admit that they share it these days. Until a century ago, it was almost mainstream. When the future Poet Laureate John Masefield was orphaned (his mother died giving birth and his father had a breakdown and died shortly afterwards) he came into the care of an aunt who shared this disapproval with a passion.

The young Masefield devoured books and wandered, rather as Wordsworth did, 'lonely as a cloud' around his home environs (he was born in Ledbury in Hereford, near where his older contemporary Edward Elgar was also wandering similarly lonely as a cloud – they should have got together). And the more he devoured his books, the more his aunt disapproved.

Strong measures were clearly required, and it was decided that he should be sent to sea. To prepare him for this, Masefield was sent to school on HMS *Conway*, the sail training ship and former wooden battleship *Nile*, then anchored off Birkenhead.

The three years he spent there from 1891 gave him a fascination for the sea, sea tradition and sea lore, but it certainly didn't cure him of books. This love of the sea was entrenched even further during his first seagoing position, on a four-masted barque called *Gilcruix*, which took him from Cardiff to Chile, via Cape Horn. Masefield's diary at the time recorded heavy seas, porpoises and flying fish and a rare nocturnal rainbow, but it ended all too soon, invalided home with sunstroke.

He abandoned his next ship altogether in New York Harbour at the age of seventeen, became a tramp, a barman and an employee in a carpet factory, where he saved enough money to buy the complete works of Chaucer. Back in England two years later, and through a series of happy meetings, he began to write poetry, thanks to the friendship of some of the most prominent poets of the age, on the fringes of the group that would eventually be known as the Georgian poets.

Masefield married an older woman called Constance Crommelin, introduced to him by the poet Laurence Binyon (author of the remembrance poem 'They shall not grow old as we that are left grow old') and soon there were children on the way. His work for the *Manchester Guardian* wasn't exactly lucrative. It was time to capitalise on the handful of poems that he had managed to get published.

That was where 'Sea Fever' came in. It appeared for the first time in his 1902 collection *Salt-Water Poems and Ballads.* His other famous poems like 'Cargoes' and 'Reynard the Fox' were all in the future, but this salt-water stuff sold reasonably well. Later versions changed the first line to the more familiar 'I must go down to the seas again' – originally it had omitted the word 'go'. It has a kind of mystical quality, not only able to conjure up the English love-and-hate relationship with the sea – the compelling way in which English history has intertwined itself with seafaring – but to do so in an era of semi-detached houses, ribbon development and commuter suburbs.

Somehow Masefield's poem speaks especially to the English life which gets no closer to the nautical than the garden pond in their semi. It speaks to the yearning for the wild in the commuter and the call of the running tide to those who peer out of their tower block. It is a deeply English poem, partly for the mismatch between the wildness described and the calm rhythm, which was so beautifully used in the musical version by John Ireland, but also in its prevailing melancholy. This is the English soul speaking trapped next to the office coffee machine, but still 'it may not be denied'.

Masefield managed eventually to make ends meet as a successful playwright and novelist. His children's novel *The Box of Delights* has survived, and his other adventure stories – *Dead Ned*, for example – had an obvious influence on children's writing in the great age of Puffin Books in the 1960s, but have rather slipped from view.

Masefield was never the staid conservative he seemed. One of his poems ('The Everlasting Mercy') was condemned from the pulpit, he was a supporter of women's suffrage, and he ran the amphibious ambulance during the Gallipoli campaign. Still, he managed to beat Rudyard Kipling to the post of Poet Laureate, twenty-eight years after the publication of 'Sea Fever', and held the post until his death from gangrene in 1967.

He was a great survivor of the age of Georgian poetry, a friend of W. B. Yeats who lived long enough to see flower power, and he managed to hold the post of Laureate longer than anyone apart from Tennyson. He also managed to be the first English writer to release an LP reading of his own poems (just as Tennyson was the first to be recorded).

There is something about 'Sea Fever' which speaks to a certain mood of English ennui, and the poem prefigures death rather as Tennyson's 'Crossing the Bar' does. Masefield did after all experience the vagrant gypsy life himself, and he clearly looked forward as a young man when he wrote the poem to 'quiet sleep and a sweet dream when the long trick's over'.

I must down to the seas again, to the lonely sea
and the sky,
And all I ask is a tall ship and a star to steer her
by,
And the wheel's kick and the wind's song and the
white sail's shaking,
And a grey mist on the sea's face and a grey dawn
breaking.

There is something very English about suburban semi-detached homes, and especially those built between the wars, with their generous gardens, their little garden gates and garages and their twee stained-glass front doors. There is nothing like them anywhere else in the world, the product of the desire for family homes in limited spaces.

For some reason, they have been execrated in England, and have become deeply unfashionable, despite being one of the most popular and humane types of housing built anywhere.

The English invented commuter suburbs, when the railways allowed the middle classes to live on the outskirts of towns, in suburbs which centred on the railway station and the high street.

Perhaps the apotheosis of the English style of place-making was in Ebenezer Howard's pioneering garden cities, in Letchworth and Welwyn, the pioneers of the rather less English new towns. Letchworth also developed a style all of its own, thanks to Raymond Unwin and Barry Parker and their Arts and Crafts cottage styles. It provided the English contribution to town planning, just as Howard intended.

His other scheme, which was to make sure that the land values were vested in the community, has attracted the disapproval of successive governments. English governments have always been a little suspicious of making people economically independent, in case they never work again. They are not that keen on everyone having their own garden either, yet the semi-detached was designed on precisely that basis.

Howard was a shorthand writer from the House of Commons and, when the great and the good adopted his first garden-city plan, they rather looked down their noses at him as they set up their committees to urge the government to build it. Instead, Howard set off on his bicycle, found the site for Letchworth and set to work. If you wait for the government to do it, he said, 'you will be as old as Methuselah'. That is as good a statement of English political philosophy as anyone ever made.

> Gaily into Ruislip Gardens
> Runs the red electric train,
> With a thousand Ta's and Pardon's
> Daintily alights Elaine;
> Hurries down the concrete station
> With a frown of concentration,
> Out into the outskirt's edges
> Where a few surviving hedges
> Keep alive our lost Elysium – rural Middlesex again.
>
> John Betjeman, 'Middlesex'

There we are in the middle of the north Atlantic, surrounded by small, floating pieces of ice, the ocean floor two miles down beneath the great, green, freezing ocean. The lifeboats have gone and the ship is sinking and the only other ship within sight is not responding to signals. What do you do and how do you behave?

That is the question at the heart of the English version of the *Titanic* story. It is a question of stiff upper lips and gentlemanly farewells in your dinner jacket, listening to the quiet, restrained sound of the orchestra playing 'Nearer, My God, to Thee' wafting over the icy air.

But *Titanic* is not just an English story. It was a ship built in Northern Ireland, managed by a struggling shipping line owned by an American banker, carrying passengers who certainly included the English but also Americans and, locked into the third-class dining room, a large number of Irish emigrants. The heroic story (see Chapter 17) – part of the English myth of fair play, good behaviour and women-and-children-first – is overwhelmingly one of the English upper and middle classes. It is part of their great romance with ice: just as Captain Scott's frozen body lay in the Antarctic, here was another block of ice getting revenge on those who presumed to set sail in an unsinkable ship.

The various film versions are not all English either. The original version, commissioned by Nazi propagandist Josef Goebbels, emphasised that this was the last gasp of a plutocratic class. The American version with Kate Winslet and Leonardo DiCaprio (1997) portrayed an ossified, hypocritical society about to collapse under its own contradictions, with the help of a small collision.

Only the Kenneth More version, *A Night to Remember*, maintains the English myth. It is poignant, heroic, tragic and terribly English as, one by one, the overwhelmingly heroic characters – perhaps not the chairman of the White Star Line, who jumped ship with the women and children – realise what is about to happen. They smoke their last cigars, occasionally resorting to firing a revolver in the air – there is no suicide as there was in James Cameron's film version. Though even *A Night to Remember* was based on a book by the American writer Walter Lord, so it may be more about an outsider's view of Englishness than anything truly home-grown.

Of all the great disasters at sea, each one remembered for its heroism in a different way, why does *Titanic* capture people's imagination? The answer is partly that the combination of melancholy inevitability and tragic self-sacrifice supports the English self-image. English souls beat with a twinge of excitement at the idea of going down with the ship, especially when it is clearly a symbolic disaster for a whole generation, the very class that found itself sacrificing life and limb on the front line of the trenches only twenty-eight months later.

The disaster has also become part of the peculiar relationship between the English and the sea, as if they were chained to a fearsome and tempestuous lover. We revel with horror at Captain Smith going down with his ship. We cheer on Captain Rostron steaming through the night at top speed on the *Carpathia*, to find the sea full of frozen corpses. We warm to Lightholer, the senior surviving officer, who went on to sail his small yacht over to Dunkirk to fetch the retreating soldiers off the beaches in 1940. 'We have strewn our best to the waves' unrest / To the shark and the sheering gull,' wrote Robert Louis Stevenson, who – though not English himself – caught the essence of the relationship. 'If blood be the price of admiralty, by God we have paid in full.'

> Nearer, my God, to Thee,
> Nearer to Thee!
> E'en though it be a cross
> That raiseth me,
> Still all my song shall be
> Nearer, my God, to Thee.

Sarah Flower Adams (1805–48)

SUMMER

'Literally for this,' said Edward Thomas, soil in his hand, to explain why he had joined up to fight on the Western Front. He was killed on Easter Monday 1917 by a shell, as he smoked his pipe. It was in this kind of mood that he began to write poems celebrating English life, and his most famous poem seems to start in mid-conversation: 'Yes, I remember Adlestrop'.

He explained something of his feelings about his native land in his essay 'This England', referring to himself in the Quantocks when he experienced the sense of 'home'. 'His train stopped at a station which was quite silent, and only an old man got in, bent, gnarled and gross, a Caliban; but somehow he fitted in with the darkness and the quietness and the smell of burning wood, and it was all something I loved being part of.'

Thomas presented this as a kind of spiritual experience, aware suddenly of 'all the birds / Of Oxfordshire and Gloucestershire'. But we know a little more than this about it because of his diary entry immediately before the First World War, on 28 June 1914, about his train journey from London to Dymock, via the Oxford to Worcester Express, which included the phrase: 'Then we stopped at Adlestrop.'

The poem itself was written in winter, on 8 January 1915 in fact, in the middle of an extraordinary surge of creativity – he wrote thirty-three poems between December 1914 and early February 1915, still writing under the pseudonym Edward Eastaway and pretending he wasn't actually doing it.

The problem was that Thomas was struggling with his conscience. He had been an insightful poetry critic for most of his writing career, siding usually with the Georgians – the young poetry movement represented by his friends. He had recently found that he could write poems himself. In the few short years left to him, he had written enough to carve out a proud section in the *Oxford Book of English Verse*. But his real struggle was about whether to enlist.

His nation was at war, and though he was old enough to avoid comment for not being in uniform, he didn't want to think of himself as afraid. He was agonising about whether to join his great friend Robert Frost in America or whether that might be seen, primarily by himself, as a form of escape from the Western Front. In the end, Thomas opted for uniformed life. The rest we know.

'Adelstrop' was published three weeks after he died, in the *New Statesman*. His admirer the composer Ivor Gurney said it was 'nebulously, intangibly beautiful'. This is true, and it is still hard to put a finger on its charm except perhaps that it conjures up that final summer of peace, a quiet moment in more than one way, and its absolutely simplicity has a innocence about it – and about England – that still makes it compelling a century later.

> Yes, I remember Adlestrop –
> The name, because one afternoon
> Of heat the express-train drew up there
> Unwontedly. It was late June.
>
> The steam hissed. Someone cleared his throat.
> No one left and no one came
> On the bare platform. What I saw
> Was Adlestrop – only the name

Bank holidays are English saints' days. Other European nations gave their people breaks from work to enjoy the sunshine. Even the Bank of England used to close on thirty-three religious festivals a year until 1834. After that, the English had to invent bank holidays to give themselves the occasional day off – to enjoy the drizzle, the sandy, soggy sandwiches and the experience of close proximity to everyone else having 'fun'.

Amazingly, the idea was not invented by the founders of England – by St Augustine or King Alfred – but by a Victorian scientist-politician who was looking for ways to encourage the English to evolve a little bit faster.

Sir John Lubbock had been flung into the world of scientific inquiry because he lived next door to Charles Darwin. When his father's bank ran into difficulties, and school fees became impossible, Darwin became his tutor and Lubbock became an early advocate of the theory of evolution.

But he was also a politician, and he believed that evolution had a special meaning for society: it meant that societies would evolve too. People would educate themselves. They would rise above the struggle for survival. The trouble was, their employers kept their noses to the grindstone six days a week, so self-education was endlessly delayed. What could be done?

Like his father, Lubbock was also a banker. As a politician, he knew he could not force employers to give people the day off. But, as a banker, he knew that, if the banks closed their doors, then so would the nation's businesses – and the day off would have been achieved. Hence his decision to draft a new law which closed the banks on four days a year (Easter Monday, Whit Monday, Boxing Day and the first Monday in August) so that people would have the time to rest and maybe read a bit – Lubbock was a doyen of the Working Men's College and a great lister of all the books people should read.

Christmas Day was already a day off in England, so he never included that. Nor did he include New Year's Day, which wasn't designated a bank holiday in England until 1974.

At one stroke, the nation was transformed. The first Monday in August 1871, after the Bank Holidays Act became law, saw extraordinary scenes at the London railway terminals as the crowds overwhelmed the trains available to take them to the seaside. 'The passengers were packed on decks and paddleboxes like herrings in a barrel, and so great was the hunger of the crowd on board one of the vessels that the steward declared himself to be "eaten out" in ten minutes after the vessel left Thames Haven,' said the *News of the World*.

Margate Jetty was simply blocked so far as to be impassable, whilst thousands of excursionists who came down by rail wandered along the cliffs. How many may have gone down is impossible to say. The people arrived at Cannon Street and Charing Cross for Ramsgate at 8am and it was 10 o'clock before the surprised but active officials of the South Eastern could accommodate all their customers.

Nothing was ever quite the same again, though the queues at railway stations have given away to exhausting queues around the M25 as people struggle to get away on a Friday afternoon for their extended weekends. Lovers escape by car. People propose to each other on bank holidays. People ignore the weather in their determination to have fun – and, often, they never forget it.

Harold Wilson later misused the whole idea during the sterling crisis of 1968 and proclaimed an extra bank holiday to avoid the value of sterling sinking through the floor, forcing the resignation of his foreign secretary as a result. Bank holidays can be dangerous weapons. Three years later, exactly a century after Lubbock's law, it was repealed and replaced with a new piece of legislation, the name of which is too long to detain us here. Bank holidays continue.

Lubbock himself died in 1913 and was buried in a wood near his home in the High Elms estate in Bromley. On the August bank holiday after that, his widow happened upon a family having their picnic on or near the grave. She flew into a rage and had his body moved into the churchyard at Farnborough in Kent, where he still lies. Had he been aware of it, you can't help feeling that Lubbock himself might have been rather pleased.

The original bank holidays under the 1871 Act of Parliament:

New Year's Day (Scotland)
Good Friday (Scotland)
Easter Monday
Whit Monday
First Monday in May (Scotland)
First Monday in August
Boxing Day (England and Wales)
St Stephen's Day (Ireland)
Christmas Day (Scotland, but already a traditional holiday in England)

I t is called Brighton Pier these days, but in its heyday it was always the Palace Pier, the last great pier to be built of a whole succession of English piers – the crowning glory of the English seaside resort. Many, if not most, have burned down, including Brighton's West Pier. There seems to be something particularly inflammable about English piers, but Brighton Pier carries on.

It is more than 1,700 feet in length and took more than a decade to build, opening in May 1899 before its famous Palace Pier Theatre had been completed. Halfway through its building work, in 1896, the old chain pier next door was swept away by a huge storm. Partly because of the pier, Brighton retains something of its louche reputation. It has managed to hold on to some of the sense of the glory days of the English seaside resort. It still combines an enjoyable seaside respectability with a hint of forbidden Parisian glamour. People would raise eyebrows if a Victorian gentleman said he was going to Brighton for the weekend. And the pier and its restaurants, smoking rooms and arcades, was the very heart of this temple dedicated to a particular side of Mammon – a very English, salty version of Las Vegas.

It was also the theatre, perched at the end of the pier, which was the great pinnacle of Brighton's appeal during the twentieth century. Here, from 1902 onwards, the greatest actors and music-hall stars would strut their stuff, with a summer celebrity season and a month of Christmas pantomime. Here you might rub shoulders with Arthur Askey, Tommy Trinder, Gracie Fields, Gillie Potter and (in the generation before) Little Tich, and (a generation later) Dick Emery and Morecambe and Wise, glimpsing them in their greasepaint slipping back to their digs opposite the Brighton Hippodrome. Or struggling into a taxi in their costumes to catch the last train back to London for the night.

The theatre was requisitioned by the army during the Dunkirk crisis in 1940, just as the audience was gathering for a performance. As soon as the audience had been refunded their money, the pier was blown up to prevent it being used as a hostile landing. The pier theatre did not reopen until 1946. It closed again in the 1970s and was removed in pieces in 1986 and stored ready to be rebuilt by the developers, who subsequently mislaid it, so that may be that for the theatre (this is a habit of developers and local authorities: Merton Borough Council stored stones for the medieval gateway of Merton Abbey safely, to make way for the new Sainsbury's Savacentre, and then – by a terrible error – used it as hard core).

Today, the pier is a shadow of its former self, a symbol of seaside culture and its decay, which is – in itself – terribly English.

The beautiful thing about Brighton is that you can buy your lover a pair of knickers at Victoria Station and have them off again at the Grand Hotel in less than two hours.

Keith Waterhouse

The English may live in cities (eighty per cent of them live in urban spaces), but they hanker for the countryside.

There is a rural idyll beating in the heart of the English, a hankering for a golden age that never quite was. Though they live with kerbstones and bus stops and street lights, they condemn townsfolk – as Rupert Brooke condemned the people of Cambridge as 'urban, squat and full of guile' – and feel deep down that they belong elsewhere.

Perhaps it is the frustrated gardener that inhabits every English soul. Perhaps it is the grandiose desire to direct the landscape around them. Perhaps it is because inside all of us there is a desire to emulate Capability Brown – to sit on a chair pointing to the far horizon, ordering: 'Perhaps a lake there, and a rolling hillside with sheep on the right'.

You can certainly be snobbish about his approach, and Capability Brown's critics were even during his lifetime, fulminating against the formula of belt of woodland, using the contours of the land, clumps of trees to drape their shadows across the grass, with a watery element somewhere – a stream, lake or moat, bridged by some rustic or classical bridge, semi-submerged.

You could deride it, but it worked.

The future landscape designer Lancelot Brown was born in the village of Kirkharle in 1716. He is said to have gathered the famous nickname by his habit of talking about the 'capability' of sites. But it was his own capability that really stands out, starting from a farm-house in Northumberland, working as a gardener's boy, to becoming the lord of the manor of Fenstanton, the designer of around 170 parks, and famously turning down work in Ireland because he had not yet 'finished England'.

His first landscaping work seems to have been at Kiddington Hall, near Woodstock in Oxfordshire. Then he happened to be recommended to Lord Cobham who asked his nurseryman if he could think of anyone who might help him landscape Stowe. So there he was, the assistant to the pioneer of naturalistic gardening, William Kent.

Brown also had a thriving architectural practice, remodelling country houses, which he handed on to Henry Holland, who in turn handed it to his pupil Sir John Soane.

Capability Brown was rooted in the English architectural tradition, and his style was deliberately picturesque. He famously dammed the small stream in the grounds of Blenheim Palace and half-flooded the new bridge that he built across the resulting lake. The poet Richard Owen Cambridge said that he hoped to die before Brown so that he could see heaven before he improved it (Cambridge actually survived him by twenty years).

In fact, although he was derided in his own lifetime, Capability Brown was destined to turn England into a kind of romantic heaven – to make it look rolling and lush, creating the blueprint for the quintessentially English garden. He was a nightmare for those committed to authenticity, but he was also highly successful – as the crowds which turn out to see his work in National Trust properties every weekend will testify even today.

Now there, I make a comma, and there, where a more decided turn is proper, I make a colon; at another part, where an interruption is desirable to break the view, a parenthesis; now a full stop, and then I begin another subject.

Capability Brown describing the language of landscape design to Hannah More at Hampton Court in 1782

There was a time when all English boys were told Clive of India was the most important historical figure they needed to emulate. These days, hardly anyone has heard of him. In fact, Robert Clive's life seems as if it was led purely for the edification of boys.

He was born in Shropshire in 1725 near Market Drayton, and was soon organising a protection racket among the local shopkeepers. He was in so much trouble so regularly that his father packed him off as a clerk to the East India Company in Madras. From this inauspicious start, he managed to defeat the French in battle, become governor of Bengal and be given a peerage when he returned home as the richest man in England.

One of the ironies of Clive's life was that, although he was clearly English, his career was forged and took place largely somewhere else entirely – in India. It is even more ironic, perhaps, that – despite all this – Clive couldn't stand India. 'If I should be so far blessed as to revisit again my own country, but more especially Manchester, the centre of all my wishes, all that I could hope or desire for would be presented before me in one view,' he wrote. Clive famously suffered from homesickness so badly that he tried to shoot himself twice. After one failed attempt he examined the pistol and found it was loaded and working, and thereupon decided that providence had spared his life for a reason.

Clive made his name at the age of twenty-five, with only a bookkeeper's training, leading the successful defence during the siege of Arcot with a handful of men, and earning the epithet 'heaven-born general' from William Pitt the Elder. When he defeated the French and Mughals at the Battle of Plassey, he added to the East India Company's lands an area larger than the British Isles, and laid the foundations of British rule in India. This was an extraordinary achievement, since it involved beating an army fifteen times the size of his own with the loss of just twenty men, and during the monsoon season.

He manoeuvred the French, in far greater numbers in India at the time, reorganised the East India Company's forces and attempted to reorganise the administration – putting down a mutiny by officers enraged at his ban on receiving gifts from Indians.

He had not exactly been above receiving gifts himself, and when his political enemies opened an inquiry into his conduct in India, and the way he had enriched himself, he answered in a thoroughly English way: 'I stand astonished at my own moderation,' he said. Even so, the parliamentary inquiry decided that he had wrongly enriched himself to the tune of £235,000 from Siraj ud-Daulah's treasury.

Clive's melancholia clearly continued even when he returned home, because he died at the age of only forty-nine in 1774 at his home in Berkeley Square. There was never an inquest, and the reasons for his death are disputed, but he probably killed himself, possibly by cutting his own throat with a penknife. He is buried in the church of Moreton Say in Shropshire, where he was Lord Lieutenant.

It appears I am destined for something; I will live.

Robert Clive, after his attempted suicide, 1743

'There's a breathless hush in the Close tonight – / Ten to make and the match to win,' wrote the English poet Henry Newbolt, the part-time imperialist, about his school playing field at Clifton College in Bristol. The poem went on:

> A bumping pitch and a blinding light,
> An hour to play and the last man in.

Newbolt was conjuring up his very first sight of his school, which he revered, with the white flannels in the summer and an elegiac sense of youth and peace. He also managed to conjure up something about England; unhurried, the summer evening in the air and the shadows lengthening, and the prospect of tea and cakes, and the sunkissed faces watching the sky – rather than watching the action on the pitch.

Newbolt's poem goes on to praise the schoolboy rallying the ranks in some far-off imperial adventure, when the 'Gatling's jammed and the Colonel dead', with the phrase: 'Play up, play up! And play the game.' The phrase came to mean a range of slightly contradictory things, about life as it was intended to be lived among certain classes of Englishmen, or a seriousness about life and war, or just about cricket.

Clifton Close was also the scene of another cricket moment: Arthur Collins' famous 628 not out in a school match, the biggest score ever achieved in cricket, which reached the front page of *The Times* in June 1899 as it developed over five days. Collins was killed in the First Battle of Ypres in 1914, giving Newbolt's poem added poignancy.

It was also where the great W. G. Grace was bowled out first ball, but very sensibly ignored it on the grounds that people had come to see him bat. It was where the future English Python, John Cleese, then a schoolboy, got the great Denis Compton out twice in one innings in 1958.

This kind of incident is especially valued in cricket, partly because it sets up a kind of David-and-Goliath struggle, which the English always like, and partly because it tests the English ability to control the emotions at their strongest. This isn't always effective. The inventor (or possibly reviver) of overarm bowling, a Kent cricketer called John Willes, did not last long at the top of the game. His first ball for Kent against the MCC in 1822 was overarm and therefore no-ball. He jumped on his horse and rode away, never to return to the game. It was made legal under the rules of the game in 1835, an appropriately lengthy period afterwards – perhaps the greatest tradition in cricket is that nothing much happens for a very long time.

Unusually for the contents of this book, all the evidence suggests that cricket really did originate in England, somewhere in the Home

Counties at some distant date. Despite all the efforts of cricket historians, there are no clues about exactly when it began except that the young Edward II was once recorded to have played a game called *creag*, though whether that really was cricket is anyone's guess.

The first recorded cricket match actually took place in Greece on 6 May 1676, when a group of English sailors from ships called *Assistance*, *Royal Oak* and *Bristol* went ashore and played. The big expansion of the game took place the following century, and here at last there is a Scottish connection. The father of the founder of Lord's cricket ground, Thomas Lord, who had been born in Thirsk, arrived in London some time in the 1770s to find fortune. He was keen to do so because his father had been a wealthy landowner, but had lost everything in 1745 when he raised a troop of cavalry to support Bonnie Prince Charlie's rebellion and ended up working as a labourer on one of the farms he had previously owned.

There you have it. The authentic, poignant note of nostalgia essential to all truly English accounts of cricket.

> For the field is full of shades as I near a shadowy coast,
> And a ghostly batsman plays to the bowling of a ghost,
> And I look through my tears on a soundless-clapping host
> As the run stealers flicker to and fro,
> To and fro:
> O my Hornby and my Barlow long ago!
>
> *Francis Thompson (1859–1907)*

This small French port on the English Channel is forever associated in the English mind with one of those peculiar miracles of escape that they tend to celebrate as victories. It is always given the English spelling too, rather than the French Dunkerque, as if it was a small fishing village, perhaps in Scotland. It is, in short, a muddling kind of place – if indeed 'Dunkirk' is a place at all, when it is actually a nostalgic idea.

Winston Churchill made his famous 'We shall fight on the beaches' speech on 4 June 1940 to celebrate the escape of 338,000 British and French troops from the beaches there, but even he warned that 'wars are not won by withdrawals'.

But if the English could not quite snatch victory from the jaws of defeat, the point about Dunkirk was that – at great loss, among the rearguard and the rescuing ships – a small defeat was snatched from impending disaster. It did look as though the entire British army, and all its tanks and equipment, would be captured or destroyed by the sudden Nazi advance, leaving the nation horribly exposed to invasion.

What made Dunkirk possible was Hitler's controversial Halt Order of 22 May, which stopped the advance of his tanks from crossing the defensive canals, and handed over the task of finishing off the British Expeditionary Force (BEF) to Goering's Luftwaffe. The order was sent uncoded and was picked up, so Churchill and the British government knew they might have time to build defences, pull back their troops behind the barrier and into the town, and organise some kind of rescue.

The naval planners believed they might have been able to rescue 25,000 men. In the end, over a period of a week, and thanks to the sacrifices of the Highland Division and the French rearguard, over 800 ships of all sizes managed to take off most of the BEF and a sizeable number of French troops, most of whom were transferred to Brest to carry on what turned out to be a hopeless defence of France.

The troops left by wading out to neck height in the waves and waiting all day, and they left minus their equipment. It was the little ships which captured the imagination, from pleasure steamers to fishing boats and cabin cruisers from the Thames – one of the yachts captained by the senior surviving officer from the *Titanic*, C. H. Lightholer (see Chapter 26), and many like him. It was somehow an English solution, by English heroes, and a symbol of the success of people power over an establishment which had failed so miserably either to prevent or prepare for war.

In the generations to come, when the problems become bigger and the institutions we deal with less human, the English may still look back to Dunkirk and the little ships, and think – Ah yes, that's what we truly are. There was something self-revelatory about Dunkirk, or at least there appeared to be to the English – the brilliant organisation, the individual flair, the popular uprising by small-boat masters, the anarchic pulling together, the snatching of consolation from disaster. It was, in the end, all very English.

Dunkirk statistics:

Troops evacuated from Dunkirk between 27 May and 4 June 1940: 338,226

Number of ships of allied nations taking part: 933

Number sunk: 236

Number of guns left by the BEF in France: 2,472

Number of tons of ammunition left: 76,097

Men of the BEF captured or killed during the retreat and evacuation: 68,111

Number of French troops taken into captivity when Dunkirk fell: 40,000

Merchant seamen who died during the evacuation: 126

Number of days Winston Churchill had been prime minister: 16

There is something very English about the start of an FA Cup final, and somehow reminiscent of that waiting around that seems to go with major sporting fixtures in the UK, and everywhere else. In my childhood, it always seemed to be in a packed, heaving, raucous Wembley Stadium, with its distinctive towers from the 1923 Empire Exhibition. There always seemed to be the Royal Marines band and always some celebrity – was it Harry Secombe; was it Tony Blackburn? – who would try to conduct an unwilling crowd in the first and last verses of 'Abide With Me'.

The FA Cup final isn't quite what it was. There are so many other football championships to compete for our attention, and all over the world. But there was a time when special trains carried tens of thousands of supporters of the finalists into London, to travel via the Metropolitan Line out to the stadium, arriving from before dawn on the damp paved streets of the capital. It was an era of ticket touts and terraces, beer and scarves, and brown, uncategorisable meat pies.

'Abide With Me' was a permanent fixture that began at the final between Arsenal and Cardiff City in 1927 (Welsh clubs have regularly taken part in the FA Cup, when generally speaking Scottish clubs have refused to). Communal singing used to be a major feature on the pitch before the match. In 1956, the songs included light classics like 'She's a Lassie from Lancashire' and 'Keep Right On to the End of the Road'. By the late 1960s, the crowds tended to have their own chants to sing. Perhaps little would induce them to sing the kind of songs people had sung around pub pianos a generation before.

As for the FA Cup, it dates back to the 1871–2 season, when the newly established Football Association had hit on the idea of a knockout tournament between the teams. Fifteen clubs entered, including the Scottish team Queen's Park which managed to get through to the semi-final without having to play a match, because they were all scrapped for one reason or another – mainly because of a failure to agree a venue for the games.

They managed a draw against Wanderers in London, but could not club together enough money to come back for a replay, so they had to withdraw. The first final took place at the Kennington Oval, know known as a cricket ground, and was won by Wanderers, a London club formed some years before by a group of former public schoolboys, which scored the only goal against Royal Engineers. And so the tradition had been born.

These days, there are no replays, and draws are decided after extra time in a penalty shoot-out.

Back in 1872, the trophy Wanderers won cost £20 and included a little figure of a footballer, which was why it had a nickname the 'Little Tin Idol'. It was won for the last time in 1895 at the old Crystal

Palace stadium, where FA Cup finals regularly attracted crowds of up to 100,000 to its twin railways stations. The winners that year were Aston Villa.

Five months later, the trophy was stolen from the William Shillcock football outfitters shop in Newtown Row, Birmingham. There was a reward offered of £10, but the trophy has never been found.

These days, the FA Cup finals are in Wembley again (after a brief period at the Millennium Stadium in Cardiff), which takes the ceremony back to where the final was played from 1923 to 2000 in the old Empire Exhibition Stadium.

The first year at Wembley (between Bolton Wanderers and West Ham) was the famous 'White Horse Final', called after a white police horse called Billy which pushed the over-capacity crowd off the pitch so that the match could start, forty-five minutes late. The reason for the problem was that an estimated 240,000 fans turned up for the match, squeezed inside the stadium, with another 60,000 locked outside the gates. Some say it is the biggest attendance for any non-racing sporting event in history, but this seems likely to be English hyperbole.

But despite the changes over the years, 'Abide With Me' still gets sung, by assorted celebrities and opera singers, before the teams run out onto the pitch. The FA Cup remains one of the great sporting events of the English year, even if you are not too fond of football.

Venues for FA Cup finals:

Kennington Oval
Crystal Palace
Stamford Bridge
Lillie Bridge
Wembley Stadium
Goodison Park
Fallowfield Stadium
Old Trafford
Millennium Stadium, Cardiff
(Replays were sometimes held elsewhere)

These days, fairies seem to be almost the preserve of Hollywood, or maybe some leprechaun-infested corner of Tralee. Alternatively, there is a sense maybe that they are some aspect of a hidden, fearsome Transylvanian creature of the night. Yet fairies were once so much part of the English psyche that the historian Ronald Hutton has called them the 'British religion'.

It is hard to overestimate just how unfashionable fairies have become in the UK during the twentieth century. They had a good start thanks to the combined Edwardian talents of Arthur Rackham and J. M. Barrie. *Peter Pan* was first shown to rapturous applause in 1904. In fact, there is some evidence that fairies tend to enjoy their revivals at the turn of centuries (*A Midsummer Night's Dream* 1595/6, Coleridge's 'Songs of the Pixies' 1793, the film *The Fairy Tale* 1997). But something about the whole Tinkerbell thing – the delicate femininity, the questionable childish sexuality – did not mix well with the century to come.

When Arthur Conan Doyle published his Cottingley fairy photographs in 1920 – the very obvious fakes made by two little girls in Yorkshire – they had the very opposite effect on later generations to the one he intended. One look at the dancing gnome, or the obvious brassieres, was enough to turn fairies into a laughing stock. In fact, one of the girls maintained until she died that they had faked the photographs because nobody believed them when they *had* seen fairies.

Seven years later, a retired naval communications pioneer, Sir Quentin Craufurd, founded the Fairy Investigation Society, designed to promote serious study. Over the years, it managed to attract a number of prominent supporters, including Walt Disney and the Battle of Britain supremo Air Chief Marshal Lord Dowding, whose career was not helped by his public expressions of belief. The Fairy Investigation Society went underground in the 1970s, from where it has only just emerged.

Despite all that, something has been going on out there to bring the hopelessly unfashionable back into fashion, subtly and below the radar of the chattering classes in London. There are now whole orchestras of people describing themselves as 'fairy musicians'. There is a magazine, published in Maryland, called *Fairie*, and enough new fairy websites to fill pages of Google. There is even an American attempt to re-brand Midsummer's Day as 'Fairy Day'. There is a globalised version of fairies under revival with a very distinctive style – dungeons and dragons by way of Botticelli – and its array of small businesses offering music, books and spells. Nor are all American either.

These are not the dark fairies you might read about in Christina Rossetti's 'Goblin Market'. This is more like a glittery and diaphanous branch of the New Age. We are talking optimistic, light-bearing fairies, bringing the natural world to life. 'A man can't always *do* as he likes,' said John Ruskin in his Slade lecture 'Fairyland' in 1893, 'but he can always *fancy* what he likes.' For Ruskin, fairies were an antidote to grim reality. In a dull concrete world, which seems determined to engulf what remains of those woods and forests, some of us do long for a bit of magic.

But maybe we shouldn't wish for these things too fervently. You only have to read the descriptions in Cornish newspapers of the

1840s, of families battering or burning their children because they believed they were changelings – enchanted blocks of wood put there by fairies who had stolen the real child away – to realise that English fairies were not a source of delight; they were a source of terror. They were troublesome, amoral, capricious and dangerous and deep in the landscape, and people used to keep them at bay if they possibly could. If they ever found themselves amongst them, they were very careful not to dance with them or eat with them, for fear they would wake up a century hence.

Despite this, the modern English soul tends to follow Rudyard Kipling in *Puck of Pook's Hill* (1906), aware that the fairies are very ancient, aware that perhaps they should not have 'broken the hills' quite so enthusiastically, but sensing also that their fairies are in some way a repository of a magical English tapestry of history. They are also careful not to recite *A Midsummer Night's Dream* three times on Old Midsummer's Day (24 June).

> 'Oh,' cried Lizzie, 'Laura, Laura,
> You should not peep at goblin men.'
> Lizzie cover'd up her eyes,
> Cover'd close lest they should look;
> Laura rear'd her glossy head,
> And whisper'd like the restless brook:
> 'Look, Lizzie, look, Lizzie,
> Down the glen tramp little men.'

From 'Goblin Market', Christina Rossetti (1830–94)

For generations, the English averted their eyes from the peculiarities of Glastonbury Tor, the strange island crowned by the tower of St Michael's Church, jutting out of the Somerset Levels. It was too weird to be quite polite. It was also the site of the hanging, drawing and quartering of Richard Whiting, the last abbot of Glastonbury, and people tended just to leave it at that.

It has never been quite clear what the new spirit was that gripped the English in the 1960s, but it has made Glastonbury – with its half-forgotten, ruined abbey – the capital city of the New Age. Not quite the New Jerusalem, but a gentle English, mythic version of it. Partly this was a renewed fascination with King Arthur and the mythology of the nation, partly a reaction against the chimera of technological progress, partly a growing interest in non-mainstream spirituality. Whatever it was, from the calm of Chalice Well to the last vegetarian tea shop, Glastonbury is now the pulsating heart of something else. It is also the presiding genius of the annual, world-famous Glastonbury Festival.

The tor is at the centre of two important legends. The first is that this is where Joseph of Arimathea landed when he bought the crown of thorns and the Holy Grail – the cup used by Jesus at the Last Supper – to these shores, and where legend has it he also brought Jesus as a boy (see Chapter 37). It is here where he buried his staff or the crown of thorns itself, and it grew into the Glastonbury Thorn, said to flower twice a year at Christmas and Easter, which eventually fell victim to a Puritan fanatic in the seventeenth century.

That is the first legend. The second is that Glastonbury Tor marks the entrance to the world of Faerie, the Avalon where King Arthur was taken to be healed of his wounds and where his coffin and bones were found by monks in 1170, and buried in state by Edward I a century later. This is the source of the idea of the 'Once and Future King' (*Rex quondam, rexque futurus*), because that was the inscription said to have been found in Arthur's tomb.

There are other legends. One idea, introduced by the mystic writer Katharine Maltwood, is that the Tor is the heart of a giant zodiac built into the hedgerows over the Glastonbury area. The slight difficulty is that the area surrounding the Tor was under water, and navigable, during the period Maltwood said it was etched out.

Either way, Glastonbury itself has begun to come back to life over the past generation, thanks to very English individuals like Wellesley Tudor Pole, the founder of Chalice Well Gardens, and the man Winston Churchill asked to organise a psychic barrier against the invading Nazis in 1940. There is a mind-expanding quality to the place, and clues about the true nature of England if we could but discern them. But this may be an over-romantic view – there are certainly those among the English who would happily build a bypass to the A303 slap through the middle.

There is on the confines of western Britain a certain royal island, called in the ancient speech Glastonia, marked out by broad boundaries, girt round with waters rich in fish and with still-flowing rivers, fitted for many uses of human indigence, and dedicated to the most sacred of deities.

St Augustine of Canterbury

William Blake was an English mystic, a misunderstood poet and a maverick artist. He also claimed a privileged ability to glimpse other worlds. He saw an angel in a tree in Peckham Rye, of all places. He saw his brother's soul leaving his body on his deathbed, clapping its hands with joy. He was haunted by peculiar apparitions, like the ghost of a flea. And he also believed he conversed at night with the great, dead poets and artists of England.

The year 1804 marked a series of breakthroughs in industrial Britain, such as Richard Trevithick's first steam locomotive and gas lighting at the Lyceum Theatre in London. Sometime that year – we don't know when – there he was, sitting in his cramped room in South Molton Street near Oxford Street in London, now the haunt of fashion houses and hairdressers with extraordinary prices, penning the words for the poem we know as 'Jerusalem'.

The poem included its famous admonition to build 'Jerusalem / In England's green and pleasant land'. Unsure what to do with it, he slipped it some years later into the long poem 'Milton' that he believed he had taken down in dictation, not just from Milton himself, but from a range of other giants from beyond the grave, at the rate of up to thirty lines at a time, 'even against my will'.

It was an exhausting and painful process, and he found himself forced to scribble pages of fantasy in the middle of the night, time after time, while his wife Catherine got up and sat with him motionless to support him in his own mental fight.

Where do you see these people, asked one acquaintance a little sceptically? 'Here, madam,' said Blake, tapping his forehead.

'Jerusalem' has become one of the best-known poems in the English language, transformed into a soaring patriotic anthem with music by Sir Hubert Parry. It is still sung by socialists and conservatives alike, partly because the words are obscure enough to satisfy everybody, partly because the tune is stirring enough to have emerged as an alternative national anthem. So patriotic, in fact, that it was banned recently from St Paul's Cathedral on the grounds that it is too nationalistic, which wasn't really what Blake meant.

The poem which begins 'And did those feet in ancient time' refers to a legend that Jesus himself had come to England as a boy. Like Milton, Blake thought that God had reserved England for special work for the world, to lead the world out of rationalism to a new age of imagination and truth. His next long poem was also called 'Jerusalem' and he had another go at it:

> And now our time returns again:
> Our souls exult, & London's towers
> Receive the Lamb of God to dwell
> In England's green & pleasant bowers.

Blake was almost incomprehensible to his contemporaries. The Poet Laureate Robert Southey called him 'a decided madman'. It wasn't for another century that 'Jerusalem', and its attack on the 'dark satanic mills' would be dusted down and rehabilitated for a new use – to inspire people to dedicate the war effort, during the First World War, to something more high-minded.

The song was borrowed by the Christian socialist campaigner Stewart Headlam and used across the front of his journal *Church Reformer*, and it was this which brought what was otherwise rather an obscure verse to people's attention. From there, it came to be noticed by the high-minded movement Fight for Right, launched by the explorer Sir Francis Younghusband in 1915. The Poet Laureate Robert Bridges was searching for some kind of song to be sung at their rally at Queen's Hall in London on 28 March the following year, where he was giving the opening address, and sent the words of 'Jerusalem' to his friend Sir Hubert Parry. Parry wrote the music in one day (10 March 1916) and gave it to the organist Walford Davies, who was conducting the choirs at the same rally. Parry pointed speechlessly to the notes of 'O, clouds unfold!' as somehow expressing something that was hugely important to him. The tune brought the house down.

Fight for Right unravelled in 1917 in in-fighting between the jingoists and the idealists, but one of the people at the rally a year before had been the pioneer feminist Millicent Fawcett. She wanted a song for her rally in 1918 to celebrate women finally winning the vote, and even persuaded Parry to conduct it (a few weeks before he died). It has been associated with women's causes, and the Women's Institute in particular, ever since.

The song has always gone beyond that, representing a yearning that is both patriotic and also spiritual, a combination that some nationalities sometimes find strange. But then the English have always needed not just to win, but to have been right – and to combine their radicalism with a deep, nostalgic conservatism.

King George V, a deeply conservative man in almost every other respect, said he preferred the song to 'God Save the King'.

Bring me my bow of burning gold
Bring me my arrows of desire
Bring me my spear: O, clouds unfold!
Bring me my chariot of fire!

I will not cease from mental fight,
Nor shall my sword sleep in my hand,
Till we have built Jerusalem
In England's green and pleasant land.

William Blake, 1804

When you watch Morris dancers, their bells jingling, their weird instruments wailing, and their heavy footsteps thundering past you, you might reasonably imagine that this was a typically English scene, a great peasant tradition and an ancient series of steps. The thought of men in white, dancing with handkerchiefs, is certainly strange enough to be English. So is the continuing friendly disputes between rival Morris organisations – like the Morris Federation or the Morris Ring – about whether men should dance alone, or women should dance alone, or both should dance together.

In fact, like many traditions which seem to be cornerstones of English life, nobody really knows the origins of Morris dancing. There is some evidence that it arrived in England sometime during the Renaissance, via Italian dancers. There is other evidence that the word originally derived from 'Moorish', at a time when Moorish decorations were suddenly fashionable. It may therefore be that, even if the Morris dancers were dramatising an English tradition, the bells on their ankles used to make them seem exotically foreign. The truth is that nobody really knows, but English peasants were adept at Morris dancing by the time that Oliver Cromwell arrived to disapprove in the 1640s.

There are two key dates in the development of Morris dancing. The first is 1448, which marks the first recorded Morris dancer in England. The second is much more precise. It is Boxing Day 1899, when the young musician Cecil Sharp first saw Morris dancers in action in Headington in Oxford, and it changed his life. Sharp was thrilled by the rhythm and learned a great deal from the musician William Kimber who was accompanying the dancers. Thinking about the experience later, he decided he would start collecting these dances, and set about doing so.

It was the great age of the folklore collector. Young men with pasty faces were soon swarming through the rural areas of England collecting stories, and – thanks to Sharp – songs and dances. Sharp cut his collecting teeth in the villages of Somerset, just as Ralph Vaughan Williams was collecting tunes in Norfolk, Sussex and Surrey. Sharp founded the Folk Dance Society in 1911 and was already publishing his songbooks for schools, carefully removing all the bawdy double entendres. The education system might shun anything of the kind these days, but the combined efforts of Cecil Sharp and Lord Baden-Powell around the Scouting camp fire, inserted English folk songs back into the national consciousness.

The real revival of Morris dancing came in the 1960s, when hundreds of new troops of dancers began to emerge, developing their own traditions, loosely based on those in their area, and occasionally given depth by the memories of the oldest generation who could just remember dancing in their youth.

A Morris-dance typology:

Cotswold Morris, dances from Gloucestershire and Oxfordshire
with hankies and sticks

North-West Morris, developing out of mill life a century ago

Border Morris, emerging from the Welsh borders and often danced
with blackened faces

Molly Dancing, mainly from Cambridgeshire

Rapper Dancing, from Northumberland with long poles

Longsword Dancing, from Durham Yorkshire with long metal
'swords'

s there anything that feels as English as the National Trust? There is something overwhelming about the combination of the friendly chintz patterned cushions, the locally made honey, the tea shops manned by unpaid volunteers, the implacably white faces, the combination of green populism and old-fashioned snobbery.

There are many ways in which the Trust is a kind of sleeping English government-in-waiting. It is already equipped with an economic policy, and more members than all the UK political parties combined. All it lacks is a foreign policy, and that can't be long in coming. The National Trust is, in short, a power in the land, and very much more than the home for retired English gentlefolk that it has sometimes been made out to be. It also seems to be discovering some of its radical roots.

The radicalism was, in some ways, the inheritance of the origins of the National Trust. It was the child of an alliance between two great reformers, the art and social critic John Ruskin and the housing pioneer Octavia Hill. Ruskin bought up a series of slums in Marylebone and handed them to Octavia Hill to manage in a humane way – she appointed a group of sympathetic but strong-minded women as rent collectors and set about knowing all her tenants and cajoling them into a responsible, thrifty existence.

The Trust itself emerged out of a long-running argument about preserving the Lake District from quarry railways. It was born on 12 January 1895, at a meeting of Hill, the Commons Preservation

Society solicitor Sir Robert Hunter, and the hymn-writer Canon Hardwicke Rawnsley. In 1907, it even achieved its very own Act of Parliament, with statutory powers to hold land and buildings in trust in perpetuity. Now, more than a century later, the Trust owns 1.5 per cent of the land area of England, Wales and Northern Ireland, managed via a decision-making structure based on the regions – it is a pioneer in government in that respect too.

The Trust's first property was the Alfriston Clergy House in Sussex, but its main purpose was protecting landscape, especially in the Lake District where the creator of Peter Rabbit, Beatrix Potter, was an early donor and enthusiast. It was the death duties imposed by Clement Attlee's Labour government after 1945 which finally did for the landed classes, and meant that huge numbers of stately homes and fine buildings – and the paintings and decoration inside – ended up in the care of the National Trust.

As a bastion of Englishness, the Trust has its political meltdowns about once a decade. In 1967, the row that led to regionalisation was really over the question of whether it was too focused on stately homes. Then there was the controversial decision to hand over protected land to the Ministry of Defence. Then there was the hunting debate from 1999. It is, in short, all very English.

But perhaps the real Englishness of the Trust is revealed in its 61,000 volunteers, who give up a portion of every week to tell people about ancient rooms, or guide them in car parks, or help with gardening or a range of other tasks. The National Trust is a monument to many things, but also the way that voluntarism lodges in the English soul.

You can also tell something about the concerns of the English by looking at the statistics for the most visited National Trust sites: Stourhead and Cliveden are currently running in the top three, both of them beautiful homes with even more beautiful, extensive and informal gardens attached. The Trust reveals us as a gardening nation, a nation obsessed with the divide between town and country that gardens represent. And none the worse for that.

> When I am gone, I hope my friends will not try to carry out any special system, or to follow blindly in the track which I have trodden. New circumstances require various efforts, and it is the spirit, not the dead form, that should be perpetuated . . . We shall leave them a few houses, purified and improved, a few new and better ones built, a certain amount of thoughtful and loving management, a few open spaces.
>
> *Octavia Hill, 1898*

O n 1 August 1798, in a sticky Mediterranean dusk, Horatio Nelson's Mediterranean fleet finally tracked down their French opponents at anchor in Aboukir Bay on the Egyptian coast. Nelson was determined to bring them to action, even in the gathering gloom. The English gun crews were crouching by their cannon while the French heaved their heavy armaments on to the seaward side where they expected their opponents to strike. The Battle of the Nile was about to begin.

The English commander had prepared for this battle by setting out clear rules of engagement, discussed with his captains evening after evening around his table on the *Vanguard*. The broad plan was to lay themselves alongside part of the French line and overwhelm it; the details would have to take care of themselves as circumstances arose, and he trusted his captains to interpret the plan effectively.

Nelson was no disciplinarian, and he had already gained a reputation for disobeying orders during the Battle of St Vincent. He steered out of line because he saw the chance to cut off a group of Spanish ships from the rest, and managed to capture them. His captains knew this was his style and knew that what he expected of them was not slavish obedience to detail, but enthusiastic commitment to the objective.

These regular dinners were the beginning of the trusting collegiate atmosphere Nelson managed to instill among his commanders, which gave rise to the idea of a 'band of brothers', a phrase stolen at the time from Shakespeare's *Henry V*. They were the basis of the adulation with which the English revered Nelson for the next century or so.

His victory at Trafalgar was organised on the same basis. When he unveiled his plan to the captains, some wept at the bold simplicity of it. Nelson was of course killed at the height of the battle, with the words 'Kiss me, Hardy,' addressed to his flag captain, among his final phrases. When the English personality gave way to the stiff upper lip, there was embarrassment about this. Could the great hero have been so unmanly? Could he not have said 'kismet', a Hindi and Arabic word meaning fate? The answer is: almost certainly not. Never underestimate English sentimentality.

'But there is one little admiral,' wrote the Edwardian Henry Newbolt, the patriotic author of various poems linking cricket with Gatling guns, 'We're all of us his brothers and his sons, and he's worth – oh he's worth at the very least, double all your tons and all your guns.'

Newbolt's song was written at the end of a century of total sea power, secured for England by Nelson's overwhelming victory at Trafalgar. It is a song that has embarrassing moments for audiences today, with its heroic bombast and naïve lyrics ('there are queer things that only come to sailormen'). But it ends with this verse:

I've been with him when hope sank under us –
He hardly seemed a mortal like the rest,
I could swear that he had stars upon his
    uniform,
And one sleeve pinned across his breast.

There was the Nelsonian symbol, and it was a symbol of English heroism even in his own lifetime, though he was lachrymose, over-indulgent, adulterous – not at all the British stiff upper lip – and not very tall. He was certainly a 'little admiral'.

What was it about Nelson? He certainly had a sense of destiny. He was also physically courageous, losing arms and eyes with abandon. But did he really have something else? This was the question the Board of Admiralty asked themselves as they tried to decide who should prevent Napoleon's invasion fleet arriving on English shores. Was Nelson all bravado and good luck? They asked to see his private diaries of the period in the Mediterranean, when he had been searching for the French fleet, and were convinced that he was the man for them. What made Nelson almost unique was his combination of compelling, humanitarian leadership and strategic brilliance.

There was an element of anarchy about Nelson – disobeying orders by putting his telescope to his blind eye at the Battle of Copenhagen to avoid the signal ordering him to withdraw, and founding a tradition of disobedience that was unique in the armed forces – because he expected to be trusted by his superiors just as he trusted his own men.

Which brings us back to the Battle of the Nile. One of Nelson's captains, Thomas Foley in the *Goliath*, happened to be leading the line of ships when the French came into sight. Foley ordered his men to get the battle sails ready, so that he could stay in front when the order came to get into line of battle.

So it was Foley, standing next to his helmsman, the battle ensigns flying behind him, who saw the emerging opportunity as the disposition of the French ships became clear. There they were anchored along the shore, and Foley realised that there might just be enough space to squeeze along their undefended side, between the French line and the shore itself.

It was a risky decision. Thinking fast as the battle got ever nearer, Foley grasped that the French commander Bruey's ships must have anchored with enough space to swing round at anchor as the tide changed, so there would almost certainly be enough sea to avoid running aground. But there was no time to consult anyone else. Foley steered between the French ships and the shore, leading the British line after him. Foley was rightly hailed as the hero of the victory at Aboukir Bay, of which Nelson had been the architect.

Foley knew he was allowed to take bold steps if he saw an opportunity. He was able to break with conventional thinking, and the apparent drift of his orders, and use his intuition. This was not rigid control – this was the English way.

Let me alone. I have yet my legs and one arm. Tell the surgeon to make haste and his instruments. I know I must lose my right arm, so the sooner it's off the better.

Nelson facing the inevitable after his wound on Tenerife, 1797 topian scenarios tend to be frustrating to read about. The heroes and heroines find themselves in the past, future or present, encountering a 'perfect' society, with the reason why everything turned out so perfectly gently explained to them in patient tones.

One Utopia stands out, not because it breaks the pattern but because it evokes a dreamlike journey into Ruskinian medievalism that has had a deep influence on the English psyche. It manages to be radical, futuristic and nostalgic all at the same time, as much medieval as it is Marxist, looking back to the Peasant's Revolt as much as it looks forward to the inevitable revolution.

William Morris never liked the idea of violence, and it was the gentleness, beauty and sheer craftsmanship of the Middle Ages that really inspired him. This is how he described a return to the four-teenth century in *A Dream of John Ball*:

> Moreover, as we passed up the street again, I was once again smitten with the great beauty of the scene; the houses, the church with its new chancel and tower, new-white in the moonbeams now; the dresses and arms of the people, men and women (for the latter were now mixed up with the men); their grave sonorous language. And the quaint and measured forms of speech, were again become a wonder to me and affected me almost to tears.

His most famous and influential dream was to become *News From Nowhere*, which unfolds as he sails from Kelmscott House, his home in Hammersmith, down the Thames to the original Oxfordshire Kelmscott in a remote medieval future. It follows the same themes as *John Ball* and was written in response to the frightening American utopian novel, *Looking Backward* by Edward Bellamy, which predicted an unpleasant authoritarian and militaristic future, which he neither believed in nor desired.

Morris' own predictions have not quite come to pass. We do not live in a rural London, and the Houses of Parliament are not yet a dung store. Yet in other ways, he did peer accurately into our present-day London: where salmon have returned to the Thames, where the inner cities have been cleared, where homes are simpler, and where state socialism has been tried and failed.

Morris thrived in the all-male medieval craft community. He dreamed of medieval guilds. He had already built one of his own, in the thriving Morris & Co., providing wallpaper and furniture to an increasingly affluent middle class. But *News From Nowhere* provides a glimpse of his own romantic yearnings, as he encounters a picture of empowered womanhood. 'She led me up close to the house, and laid her shapely sun-browned hand and arm on the lichened wall as if to embrace it,' he wrote, 'and cried out, "O me! O me! How I love the earth, and the seasons, and weather, and all things that deal with it, and all that grows of it – as this has done!"'

The shapely, sun-browned hand is also a bit of a clue. There is something of the erotic dream about *News From Nowhere*. The heroine is one of those powerful female characters that seem to dominate the lives of the back-to-the-land writers of the Victorian age. There was some element of erotic yearning about them. There certainly was about Morris, who married one of the great beauties of the age who embodied the pre-Raphaelite ideal of beauty, Jane Burden, but lost her to his friend Dante Gabriel Rossetti.

As he formed the words, the train stopped at his station, five minutes' walk from his own house, which stood on the banks of the Thames, a little way above an ugly suspension bridge. He went out of the station, still discontented and unhappy, muttering 'If I could but see it! If I could but see it!' but had not gone many steps towards the river before (says our friend who tells the story) all that discontent and trouble seemed to slip off him.

William Morris, *News From Nowhere (1890)*

When the young Charles II famously took refuge in the Boscobel Oak on the border between Shropshire and Staffordshire in 1651, as he escaped from the Battle of Worcester, he added a royal dimension to the idea of sturdy, enduring Englishness. There are Royal Oak pubs all over England now, and even a Tube station of the same name. There was a battleship called *Royal Oak*, unfortunately now at the bottom of the sea at Scapa Flow, where it was despatched in 1939 by U-47.

The royal-oak idea dovetailed neatly with the wooden walls of England, the oak-built ships which defended the English, not to mention 'Heart of Oak', the patriotic song penned by the actor David Garrick, which included the immortal and slightly excessive lines 'heart of oak are our ships / Heart of oak are our men'. The song was written to celebrate this 'wonderful year' (1759), where the British forces managed the military equivalent of the 2012

Olympics, with a whole series of victories, including that of Quiberon Bay.

But England is not the only country to have embraced the oak as its official national tree. The others include: Cyprus, Estonia, France, Germany, Moldova, Romania, Latvia, Lithuania, Poland, Serbia and the USA.

And you can see why. The oak is an amazing tree, supporting about 500 other species, and spread by birds – one single jay can gather and store up to 5,000 acorns in ten weeks. Its potential longevity is also downright staggering. A 1,000-year-old oak tree stands in a field at Manthorpe, near Bourne in Lincolnshire, where its hollow trunk is still used for parties. At one point, it is claimed, three dozen people managed to stand up inside it.

Nor is it alone. The Major Oak in Sherwood Forest is old enough to have sheltered Robin Hood, as old as the English language itself, as one history noted back in 1790. Or the Knightwood Oak, the tallest in the New Forest, planted around the time of the Battle of Agincourt. Or the Allerton Oak in Liverpool which used to be the venue for the local hundred court another couple of centuries before that.

There are hanging trees, from where highwaymen breathed their last. There are gospel trees and writers' trees. There are even some which were used as pubs inside their hollow trunks. There are also far fewer oaks than maybe there ought to be, mainly because of the navy – a ship like HMS *Victory* took about 2,000 of them to build.

The celebration of oak trees and the Royalist cause was linked with the development of Oak Apple Day, celebrated on Charles II's birthday on 29 May by wearing oak leaves. It was known in the West Country as Shick-Shack Day, for reasons that are now a little obscure, and turned out to be a wonderful opportunity for ragging anyone suspected of republican opinions.

This is not to be confused with Apple Day (the nearest weekend to 30 October), introduced in 1990 by the charity Common Ground, dedicated to celebrating ordinary beauty and designed to celebrate the role of apples in English culture. It manages to catch some of the spirit of Oak Apple Day without the Royalist connotations.

Sing for the oak-tree
This monarch of the wood,
Sing for the oak-tree
That growth green and good;
That growth broad and branching
Within the forest shade
That growth now; and yet shall grow
When we are lowly laid!

Mary Howitt (1799–1888)

The English are certainly not the only nation to have a penchant for loveable rogues and thieves. The Australians have Ned Kelly; the Americans have Jesse James, Bonnie and Clyde and a whole coachload of other baddies to love. But the legendary English outlaws have another quality to them, a streak of romance and generosity.

Robin Hood gave away his money to the poor. He faced down sheriffs and bishops and even Bad King John. Dick Turpin gave away his ill-gotten gains as a highwayman, a swashbuckling mythic figure who dodged officials and dashed to York to escape them on his horse Black Bess, or so it was said later. They are heroes on our side.

Both these legendary outlaws became magical touchstones for turning the existing world, and existing powers, upside down. There was a seek-him-here-seek-him-there element to them. They slip through our fingers just as they slipped through the fingers of their pursuers. They dash in and turn people's lives and luck inside out and dash out again. They are devious, riotous and overwhelmingly amoral.

In reality, Dick Turpin was a horse thief, with a pockmarked face and a record of gratuitous violence, arrested under the alias John Palmer, and hanged in his best frock coat in York in 1739. As usual for English outlaw-heroes, there is some confusion about what happened to his body – he was buried in the small church of St George in York, but a mob dug him up three days later and carried him away to save him from the anatomists.

The real-life Robin Hood is much more elusive. His first mention in literature was in 1377 in William Langland's classic *Piers Plowman*, where a drunken priest criticises himself for knowing the rhymes of Robin Hood better than he knows his prayers.

The legend itself is much older than that. An English troubadour, Adam de la Halle, wrote a song in the 1260s called 'Jeu de Robin et Marion'. By then the legend must have been so widespread that many people were nicknamed 'Robinhood', and not all of them criminals.

When the historians started to write about him in the sixteenth century, he was reported as having been born in 1160 in Loxley – in Yorkshire or Nottinghamshire or possibly even Warwickshire – and been called Robert Fitzooth. He was also supposed to have used the title, perhaps ironically, of the Earl of Huntingdon.

He died, so the story goes, at Kirklees Monastery on 18 November 1248 at the age of eighty-seven. In 1690, his gravestone was still in what had been the monastery grounds, with an almost indecipherable inscription – in spelling unknown to antiquarians. It said:

> Hear undernead dis laitl stean,
> Laiz Robert earl of Huntingtun.
> Near archir ver az hie sa geud
> And pipl kauld im Robin Heud.

His sidekick Little John was supposed to have been exiled to Ireland, though there was also a grave claimed to be his in Hathersage in Derbyshire. The grave was opened in 1764 and a thirty-inch thigh bone taken out, which was put in the window of the home of the parish clerk. It was stolen from there by the antiquarian Sir George Strickland.

Unfortunately for Robin Hood's gravestone at Kirklees, the earth had not actually been disturbed underneath it and most of the stone disappeared in the nineteenth century, despite Victorian railings, because the navvies working on the Yorkshire & Lancashire Railway believed that fragments from it could cure toothache. It was a fake.

Since then, the hunt for the original Robin Hood has been almost as intense as it was in the stories. The most promising name in the legal records was a fugitive in the Yorkshire assize rolls for 1225/6 called Robert Hod or Hobbehod, who may also have been the hanged outlaw Robert of Wetherby. The man who hunted him down, Eustace of Lowdham, had been deputy sheriff of Nottingham, and later became the sheriff. There was also a Robert FitzOdo from Loxley who was stripped of his knighthood in the 1190s. The sheriff of Nottingham from 1209 to 1224, Philip Mark, was known for his own robberies, false imprisonments and seizure of land.

But for all the work of historians, the story of Robin Hood will always be related to the peculiar period when the king of England, Richard the Lionheart, was in prison in Austria and Germany, and a vast ransom was being collected in silver in the crypt of St Paul's Cathedral to pay for his release.

This explains some of Robin's talismanic properties – a lonely, loyal struggle on behalf of the true king, battling against his corrupt officials. Similarly, the leaders of the Peasants' Revolt in 1381 regarded themselves as loyal subjects of Richard II, fighting in just the same way against his corrupt placemen.

The Robin Hood legend implies a kind of millenarian hope that the king would return, like Odysseus to Ithaca or Christ to the temple – cleansing and righting wrongs. 'I love not man in all the worlde / So well as I do my King,' says Robin in an early version of the ballad.

It is a legend that says the world is upside down, radical in an English populist way, which is why it still has resonance today.

How hath the knyght his leue i-take,
And wente hym on his way;
Robyn Hode and his mery men
Dwelled styll full many a day.

Lyth and lysten, gentil men,
And herken what I shall say,
How the proude sheryfe of Notyngham
Dyde crye a full fayre play.

From the 'Gest of Robyn Hode', c.1460

R evolutionaries have always found England a frustrating place. They waited on tenterhooks for revolt to spread during the 1926 General Strike, only to find that bored trade union pickets were playing football with the police. This peculiarity goes right the way back – to the Peasants' Revolt in 1381 and probably before.

In 1381, the peasants were stirred up by the tensions generated by the Black Death, and the high taxes to pay for the Hundred Years War with France. Their demands seemed pretty radical: lower taxation and changes in the regulations about labourers' pay. Equally radical was the preaching of John Ball and the other leaders, Jack Straw, Wat Tyler and the rest, whose names still echo down the centuries; as was their behaviour, breaking into the Tower of London and murdering the Archbishop of Canterbury. But once they got to Smithfield, there was no question of overthrowing the boy king, Richard II. On the contrary, the peasants regarded themselves as his loyal subjects. It was the king's corrupt officials they wanted to dismiss.

It was the bankers they hated, aspiring to recreate the ancient equality of Anglo-Saxon rule. Those were the slogans shouted by the peasants, innkeepers, clergymen and farmers who burst into London on 13 June 1381, tearing down John of Gaunt's Savoy Palace in the Strand, hunting down lawyers and Flemish traders. Those storming through Aldgate and across the Thames shouted the slogan 'with Richard and the true commons'.

This needs some investigation. Similar rebellions on the Continent were carried out by semi-terrorists, and it may be that there was a distinction between radicalism in England and continental Europe, at least in southern Europe, where revolutionaries owed their ideas to the so-called Manichean heresy. The English gentry did not pine – as the continental gentry so often did – for urban living. They settled in the countryside. When the countryside rose up against the town, as it did in England too, this was not necessarily the poor against the rich – it was the powerless against the powerful, those who grew vegetables against those who grew money. Even the records of those punished for their involvement in the Peasants' Revolt include a number of well-to-do country types, yeomen farmers, clergymen and tradesmen.

The intellectual descendant of the revolutionaries of 1381, and of Wat Tyler – stabbed by the mayor of London in Smithfield where he was then executed – was William Morris (see Chapter 41). In 1886, he imagined dreaming his way back to the revolt, and meeting John Ball himself in a church in the middle of the night, and talking about the past and future. And afterwards, he said that he 'pondered all these things, and how men fight and lose the battle, and the thing that they fought for comes about in spite of their defeat, and when it comes turns out not to be what they meant, and other men have to fight for what they meant under another name'.

This is typically melancholic, but it is also wise, in a distinctively English way. That is the way change happens in England, round and round. It is in some ways the ultimate English antidote to revolutionary change.

> When Adam delved and Eve span,
> Who was then the gentleman?
>
> *John Ball*

'It is a truth universally acknowledged, that a single man in possession of a good fortune must be in want of a wife.' So begins Jane Austen's *Pride and Prejudice*, considered by many to be England's greatest novel. The constant film adaptations, TV series and novel sequels seem to fuel our obsession still further. Perhaps this affection was sparked to some extent by Andrew Davies' hugely successful BBC adaptation (1995) with Jennifer Ehle as Elizabeth Bennet and Colin Firth as Mr Darcy.

Jane Austen herself was on the reserved side and might be taken aback by the current Austen-mania. She was born into a large and slightly impoverished rectory at Steventon in Hampshire, and lived her life surrounded by hordes of largely impoverished younger cousins. The plight of English women from the minor landed gentry dependent on marriage for financial security, and the intricate economics and interplay between the social divisions were some of her major themes.

Austen died in 1817 and her grave in the nave of Winchester Cathedral mentions her name but not the novels that made her world famous after her death. She published only six – *Sense and Sensibility* (1811), *Pride and Prejudice* (1813), *Mansfield Park* (1814), *Emma* (1815), *Northanger Abbey* (1818, posthumous), and *Persuasion* (1818, posthumous) – most anonymously (attributed as 'By a Lady'), and struggled with *Pride and Prejudice* for years under the title *First Impressions*.

She did acquire a fashionable following in the royal family, and there was some favourable comment by reviewers, of which two in particular helped make her reputation – Sir Walter Scott, the great Scottish novelist, and Richard Whately, the Archbishop of Dublin, a man who had shocked polite society by preaching to Queen Victoria with his leg resting on the top of the pulpit.

As everyone English knows, *Pride and Prejudice* concerns the adventures of a young lady called Elizabeth Bennet, the second of five sisters, her hysterical mother and her laid-back, rather cynical lazy father. It describes how she thoroughly misjudges Mr Darcy, through a series of misunderstandings, especially after his disastrous first, rather snobbish, proposal of marriage – thinking him haughty and cruel. By the end of the book, however, she finds he is quite the reverse – much to the horror of his relative Lady Catherine de Bourgh.

What Jane Austen achieves is an extremely funny novel that keeps you on the edge of your seat, yet centres not on an exotic adventure but on the very ordinary business of finding someone to love. Her enemies, as always, are snobbery, money and pretension.

Jane Austen died at the age of forty-one, and never married.

That will do extremely well, child. You have delighted us long enough. Let the other young ladies have time to exhibit.

Mr Bennet discourages his daughter Mary from playing the piano again

That's the way to do it! Even these days, when Punch and Judy shows are comparatively rare, and even strings of sausages are a bit of a surprise, we understand where that injunction comes from. We also know it is spoken with a strange, raucous nasal voice, and with gusto and self-satisfaction, the very essence of the phrase 'as pleased as Punch'.

There is something about Punch and Judy shows, with their casual murders and multiple brutalities, which English children seem to love – not to mention the policeman, the crocodile and the sausages. With its striped red and white booths, it almost smells of ice cream, jelly and the seaside.

But, like many English institutions, the origin of Mr Punch is actually Italian. He derives from the *commedia dell'arte* and the Italian Renaissance, a direct descendant of the character Pulcinella, and he owes as much to the presence of itinerant Italian players in the sixteenth century in London as to anything else. Samuel Pepys saw his first Punch and Judy show, thanks to an Italian called Pietro Gimonde, in Covent Garden on 9 May 1662. He described it as 'an Italian puppet show'.

And at that stage, and throughout the raucous eighteenth century, Punch and Judy was indeed a marionette show. It was only in Victorian England that Punch became a glove puppet, which allowed him to wield his stick with even more ferocity. He also shifted his audience from adults to children. In fact, the more knockabout Punch became, the more he shifted to audiences who really appreciate that kind of humour.

At the same time, he also tended to lose some of his really dark fellow characters, like the Hangman and the Devil. Toby the Dog, who used to be played by a real dog in the original performances, has also tended to bow out.

The plot is variable and barely exists anyway beyond a number of encounters between Mr Punch and the law, and sometimes supernatural forces too. He is as outrageous as Don Giovanni, as violent as Dick Turpin, but he always wins through. No wonder he was as pleased as Punch. He fits neatly into the category of English rogues, with bizarre seventeenth-century dress and, perhaps also, a strong Italian accent.

Judy. Where's the baby?

Punch. (In a melancholy tone.) I have had a misfortune; the child was so terrible cross, I throwed it out of the winder.
(Lemontation of Judy for the loss of her dear child. She goes into asterisks, and then excites and fetches a cudgel, and commences beating Punch over the head.)

Punch. Don't be cross, my dear: I didn't go to do it.

Judy. I'll pay yer for throwing the child out of the winder. (She keeps on giving him knocks of the head, but Punch snatches the stick away and commences an attack upon his wife, and beats her severely.)

Judy. I'll go to the constable, and have you locked up.

From Henry Mayhew's collected script (1851)

magine the scene. We are on the seafront at a famous seaside resort, under a partially covered bus shelter, peering out at the sea. The inexorable waves are breaking on the shingle before us, but the distance is obscured by the mist, and the drizzle from it is splashing into our faces.

We hold our hands underneath our packages of warm fish and chips, sprinkled with salt and vinegar, to stave off the cold. It isn't supposed to be like this in August, we say to ourselves, outraged and yet patiently accepting.

In front of us, on the stones, some hardy souls are wrapped against the wind in colourless anoraks up to their throats, protected from the worst of the weather by joyful-looking windbreaks flapping incessantly as they try to fly free of the stakes hammered deep into the sand.

Is that someone swimming, we ask, surprised, reaching for the first taste of the warm chips and the taste of salt on the tongue. It isn't. But we are having fun, aren't we. Aren't we?

I don't know if we were or not, but we could have consoled ourselves that we were having a traditional English experience, recognisable to our parents and their parents before them and probably – notwithstanding global warming – our children and their children after them.

The English penchant for the seaside began relatively late, when a doctor called Richard Russell published a tract called *A Dissertation concerning the Use of Sea-water in Disease of the Glands.* It was 1750, and the idea of water being health-giving had caused crowds to descend on the various spa towns in the high season. Russell diverted some of them to the seaside, and got a head start himself by moving to the small Sussex village of Brighthelmstone.

It was a prescient move. Within a generation, Brighton – as it was called by then – was booming. By 1820 it had a Royal Pavilion and a population of 24,000. And accelerating the growth of seaside resorts were the Napoleonic Wars, which meant that the well-to-do had to holiday at home rather than on the rather risky Continent.

Then steamships became synonymous with seasides. Ferries took 95,000 people from London to Margate and back in 1830. Then it was the train. Then it was motor coaches, turbocharged by the special excursion ticket prices between the wars and by the advent of paid holidays. Later still, it was the motorscooter, when no bank holiday was complete without some kind of riot in Brighton between mods and rockers.

The seaside world has seriously declined in recent decades, thanks to foreign holidays and package tours to Lanzarotte. The old land-ladies died out, the Fawlty Towers hotels went the way of Fawlty Towers, the piers caught fire or fell to bits, the old pier-end comedians turned their toes up. The old resorts became more divided in class terms – Blackpool and Margate were working class, Brighton and Southport middle class. Lyme Regis and a handful of others have verged on something else, with Italian salads with pancetta available on the beaches of Dorset at steep prices.

And in its way, this was very English too. But the peeling bus shelters and tacky nightclubs, and that seaside stench of decay, was perhaps the underside of England we prefer to ignore.

You think Margate more lively. So is a Cheshire cheese, full of mites, more lively than a sound one; but that very liveliness only proves its rottenness. I remember, too, that Margate, though full of company, was generally filled with such company as people who were nice in the choice of their company were rather fearful of keeping company with. The *hoy* went to London every week, loaded with mackerel and herrings, and returned loaded with company. The cheapness of the conveyance made it equally commodious for dead fish and lively company. So, perhaps, your solitude at Ramsgate may turn out another advantage.

William Cowper (1731–1800)

Sometime between 1859 and 1865, when England was undergoing the most rapid change in history, a Birmingham solicitor called Harry Gem and his Spanish friend Augurio Perera combined the best of rackets and the best of pelota – a Spanish ball game – to create tennis. They played it on a croquet lawn at Edgbaston. When they moved to Leamington Spa in 1872, they took the game with them and founded the first tennis club in the world. The following year, a Welsh major, Walter Wingfield, patented a similar game borrowing the rules of real tennis, which he called Sphairistike (from the Greek adjective meaning 'relating to ball games'), which became known as 'Sticky'.

The development of tennis, and especially Wimbledon (see Chapter 50), seems to have gone hand in hand with the development of the peculiarly English delicacy of strawberries and cream. It tastes not just of a green, pollen-filled English summer but of deuce and the thwack of ball on racket. The Wimbledon tournament manages to get through more than twenty-three tonnes of strawberries and 7,000 litres of cream.

The connection between strawberries and cream and tennis seems to stretch back to Thomas Wolsey, the cardinal who built Hampton Court, the Tudor venue for real tennis. It was he who made the original pairing, serving them from the beginning of the sixteenth century.

Strawberries and cream did not save Wolsey from the displeasure of Henry VIII, who got his hands on Hampton Court. But from the very first Wimbledon tournament in 1877, strawberries and cream were what they served.

Prices of strawberries and cream portions at Wimbledon:

1990, £1.60
1995, £1.75
2000, £1.80
2005, £2.00
2010, £2.50
2014, £2.50

There has always been a very English kind of magic surrounding Shakespeare, and all sorts of superstitions. It has resulted in actors fearing to quote *Macbeth* too enthusiastically, especially in theatres, and to refer to it by euphemisms as the Scottish Play or the Bard's Play. Rudyard Kipling imagined three children 'breaking the hills' and reviving the fairy Puck, or Robin Goodfellow, from wherever he was resting, just by performing *A Midsummer Night's Dream* on Midsummer's Day. Shakespeare's witches' spell in Macbeth is supposed to have been borrowed from contemporary witches.

And then there is *The Tempest*.

This involves a magician called Prospero and the 'airy spirit' Ariel he conjures up to help him. It is Ariel in Act V who sings the song 'Where the bee sucks', perhaps the most English and the most memorable of all Shakespeare's songs – especially when it is set to music, as it has been by many composers, but specifically by Thomas Arne – who also wrote the music for the bombastic 'Rule, Britannia'.

Where the bee sucks – with its descriptions of lying under cowslips – ought to be a kind of pastoral national anthem.

Where the bee sucks, there suck I:
In a cowslip's bell I lie;
There I couch when owls do cry.
On the bat's back I do fly
After summer merrily.
Merrily, merrily shall I live now
Under the blossom that hangs on the bough.

Something happens to the English, and perhaps especially the English middle classes, in that period between June and July that is most heady with excitement, when low summer shifts to high summer. They start reaching for their picnic hampers and feeling a little sporty. And when it isn't the Henley Regatta, when the middle classes parade with blazers, Leander ties and white trousers which used to fit them in their youth, it has to be Wimbledon that captures the imagination. In fact, it dominates the way the English frame their memories of an English summertime, watching the hopeless struggles of the English players at teatime, or drinking Pimm's in the afternoon sunshine to the gentle sound of THUMP, THUMP, Thirty forty.

The very word 'Wimbledon' conjures up a spirit of luxurious hopelessness, as successions of American women or Central European men slug it out on Centre Court in white, sending the English challenger packing.

There is something erotic in an English way about the first appearance of sun on a tennis court, when – 'oh, weakness of joy', as John Betjeman described Miss Joan Hunter Dunn – the gentlemen eye the ladies and vice versa.

Wearing white is de rigueur. It is actually in the rules, and the rules of Wimbledon are pretty strict. There are regular spats about them; in fact my great-grandfather – the sports journalist and croquet champion Bonham Carter Evelegh – walked out of his job as chief umpire over a flagrant defiance of the rules on the size of tennis balls. Wimbledon remains a caricature of itself when it comes to decorum. Even in the 1970s, they were still listing the women's champion Chris Evert on the scoreboards as 'Mrs J. M. Lloyd'. In the 1980s, they were calming the court antics of John McEnroe by calling him 'Mr'.

Of course, there have always been games like tennis. The aristocracy would play real tennis, and you can still see the venue at Hampton Court, though it is more akin to archaic squash. If any one nation invented tennis scoring it was probably the French; Charles VIII died from a bang to the head at Amboise Castle in 1498 after watching a medieval tennis match, and the tennis scoring system borrows partly from the French and partly, it seems, from the ancient Sumerians.

The Sumerian civilisation, in ancient Babylon about 3,300 BC – even before Stonehenge – was ruled day to day by a caste of accountant-priests, a fearsome combination of roles that included blessing and counting. For them, the key magical number – the equivalent to our hundred – was sixty. Everything counted up to sixty, came in bundles of sixty or in fractions of sixty, which appears to be the basis of the strange tennis scoring system: the score implies that sixty is the score after forty. Chivalric slang used the word 'egg' – or '*l'oeuf*' in French – to mean 'nothing'. That's why the word 'love', which sounds just like it – a chivalric joke – is used to mean 'no points'. The French don't appreciate the joke. They use the word 'zero' in tennis.

By the 1870s the All England Croquet Club was up and running in Worple Road in Wimbledon. It subsequently changed its name and purpose to include tennis, and passed the motion to launch the first lawn tennis championship. Wimbledon was born in July 1877 and 200 spectators came to see the first ever Wimbledon champion, rackets player Spencer Gore, thrash his opponent W. C. Marshall 6-1, 6-2, 6-4. They paid a shilling each for the privilege.

The club moved to its present site in 1922, and the television cameras arrived in 1937. Centre Court remains the focus, especially after they built the retractable roof which takes twenty minutes to shut, ending the dodgy relationship with the weather – at least for the main matches. But it is No. 2 Court where the unexpected happens, and where John McEnroe, Pete Sampras, Serena Williams and Maria Sharapova have all found themselves unexpectedly knocked out.

At the north end of the grounds, there is now a huge television screen, visible from a grass mound which was originally christened Henman Hill. It is now known as Murray Mound, but Andy Murray – as everyone knows – is actually Scottish.

Thanks to Wimbledon, lawn tennis has been given to the world. It remains recognisably English perhaps only in the Wimbledon tradition and in the strange atmosphere of relaxed carnival frivolity that comes over the English when Wimbledon is on our screens.

They act like they've got the biggest tournament in the world, and they're right, they do.

Pete Sampras on the All England Club

There is something wonderfully redolent of the English middle classes about *The Wind in the Willows*, and in A. A. Milne's stage version of it, *Toad of Toad Hall*. Toad is vain, delusory and obsessive, but he is apparently preferable to the yobs in the Wild Wood who take over his house for drinking and carousing. Toad, Badger, Rat and Mole cut and slash their way back and society is saved. We breathe a big sigh of relief.

Kenneth Grahame, one of the great children's writers of the twentieth century (though he was actually born in Edinburgh), wrote the story for his son Alastair, for whom he invented the characters in a series of letters. The book was published in 1908 and was an immediate success. Grahame had left his job as Secretary of the Bank of England and went to live in Cookham in Berkshire, next to the Thames, where he had been brought up. (There are various stories about why he left the bank, which may have had something to do with a shooting incident there.)

Alastair was never well, was blind in one eye and threw himself in front of a train around his twentieth birthday. A kind of sadness, at least mild nostalgia, pervades the whole business. But there is a kind of happier sense of memory as well. When Ratty describes messing around in boats, that was pretty much what Grahame did most of the time.

Perhaps that was why he was never recorded as having met Cookham's other great creative product at the time, the artist Stanley

Spencer, whose religious fantasies also bring the river and the Thames Valley to life. Kenneth Grahame was a deeply conservative man and Stanley Spencer was in a peculiar class of his own, and a generation younger. Even so, it is a pity we know nothing about them meeting on the banks of the great river. What they have in common is this strong mystical sense of the Thames.

Christopher Robin Milne, child hero of *Winnie-the-Pooh*, describes how both his parents loved the book and it is clear how much Pooh and Piglet owe to Toad and Mole. We all owe something too because *The Wind in the Willows* is a modern fairy tale, interspersed with morality tale – plus a little bit of English nostalgic snobbery. It is a heady mix.

'Hold hard a minute, then!' said the Rat. He looped the painter through a ring in his landing-stage, climbed up into his hole above, and after a short interval reappeared staggering under a fat, wicker luncheon-basket.

'Shove that under your feet,' he observed to the Mole, as he passed it down into the boat. Then he untied the painter and took the sculls again.

'What's inside it?' asked the Mole, wriggling with curiosity.

'There's cold chicken inside it,' replied the Rat briefly; 'coldtonguecoldhamcoldbeefpickledgherkinssaladfrenchrollscresssand wichespottedmeatgingerbeerlemonadesodawater—'

Ratty explains the picnic to Mole

AUTUMN

n 1310, King Edward's II's favourite Piers Gaveston was murdered by jealous barons. When they went through his belongings, they discovered a fork. The fact that we know this is some evidence of their rage, and just how much they believed the discovery of anything quite so continental, fashionable and downright camp as a fork seemed to justify his dispatch.

This is, of course, a strangely English idea, and there has always been a boneheaded element in the English character that believes itself to be a bastion of sanity and a check on encroaching effeminacy. That is what did for Piers Gaveston.

The story is also a reminder that, before the trend caught on in the early fourteenth century, most people had no forks. They brought their knives to the table with them and bundled stuff into their mouths with their hands. That is at least one reason that explains the favourite and traditional Anglo-Saxon concept of pies. You could hold them and put them in your mouth, and without the use of anything suspect like a fork.

But how did the great medieval savoury pie become the sweet Bakewell tart? That has very little to do with Bakewell in Derbyshire, lovely though it is, and a great deal to do with the same fashionable foreign-food trends that brought us the fork. One of the upshots of the crusades to Palestine in the 1090s was that the returning crusaders brought with them fancy eastern, originally Persian, ideas about cooking. They began adding dried fruit and spices to their pies. The pies got bigger and, once there were knives and forks, they got bigger still. They got sweeter, and soon they had merged with that great Anglo-Saxon favourite, the custard tart. And lo and behold, there was the Bakewell tart, English with extra almonds from Persia and beyond, all rolled together.

Bakewell claims to be the home of the authentic Bakewell pudding and many believe it to come originally from the Rushbottom Lane district in that town. It is said that the recipe was originally something of an accidental invention of the 1860s, the result of a misunderstanding between Mrs Graves, landlady of the White Horse Inn, and her kitchen assistant. A nobleman visiting the inn (now called the Rutland Arms) ordered a strawberry tart. Mrs Graves asked an inexperienced kitchen assistant to make one, but the assistant made a savoury pastry. The result was so successful with the guest that the recipe became recognised as a Bakewell pudding.

Mrs Wilson, wife of a tallow chandler who lived in the cottage now known as the Old Original Bakewell Pudding Shop, saw the possibility of selling the puddings commercially, managed to get hold of the recipe, and opened a business of her own. Bakewell tarts and Bakewell puddings have existed side by side ever since.

Cover a wide shallow dish with thin puff paste. Put in it a layer of jam, preferably raspberry, but any kind will do. It should be half an inch thick. Take the yolks of eight eggs and beat the whites of two. Add half a pound of melted butter and half a pound each of sugar and ground bitter almonds. Mix all well together, and pour into the pastry case over the jam. Bake for half an hour and serve nearly cold.

Recipe for Bakewell pudding by Alison Uttley, local writer,
from Recipes from an Old Farmhouse *(1966)*

For generations, the schoolchildren of England learned their history starting with the Battle of Hastings which – as almost everyone knows – was in 1066 (14 October), some six centuries before the Great Fire of London (2–5 September 1666) and some nine centuries before the English victory in the World Cup final (30 July 1966). There we are: English history at a glance.

There was Harold II, successfully obliterating one of the twin, linked invasions which threatened his rule, and marching south to deal with the second one. He tried and failed to take William's makeshift wooden castle near Hastings by surprise, and William kept his army awake all night, afraid of a night attack. He marched out at dawn the next morning to find the English drawn up on Senlac Hill near the modern town of Battle (the exact spot is still disputed).

Neither army was much more than 8,000 men and Harold's force was made up almost entirely of infantry. They are popularly supposed to have been beaten after William's knights pretended to run away and then turned on the pursuing foot soldiers. There does seem to have been a genuine panic among the Bretons, led by Alan the Red, on William's left flank and a rumour went round his army that William had been killed. But in the ensuing melee, Harold was killed – popularly by a combination of an arrow in the eye and a blow from one of William's knights. His brothers Gyrth and Leofwine died with him. All their bodies were found after the battle near the top of the hill, though there is a persistent legend that Harold survived the battle and became a monk.

Either way, William then advanced by a circuitous route on London and crowned himself king on Christmas Day. The Norman transformation of England had begun, and the language changed as a result – and it might be argued that the great divide between the defeated Saxon populace and a new Anglo-Norman aristocracy has never quite been healed.

You can still stand in the ruins of Battle Abbey, on the stone dedicated to Harold on the spot where he was supposed to have died, and look down the less challenging slopes of Senlac Hill – which have been smoothed out somewhat over the centuries – and imagine the battle that changed English history and changed the nation perhaps more fundamentally than any other event. You can, also, if you close your eyes, imagine the shouts and screams of the dying as the Saxon housecarls swung their double-headed axes so hopelessly at William's cavalry and never rose again.

But why does English history always seem to start at 1066? Certainly it emphasised the importance of the new Franco-Norman elite, and obscured the institutions and history of the Anglo-Saxon elite who had been displaced. Maybe in those days, when the ancient liberties of King Alfred were a radical English rallying cry, it seemed safer to pretend that English history began with the invasion.

It is, in short, a small plot to stop us looking too closely at the world before the current aristocracy took up their castles and stately homes. Perhaps it didn't suit our rulers' purposes either to remember just what a close-run thing the Battle of Hastings was, as in so many of the decisive battles throughout English history.

'The Saxon is not like us Normans. His manners
    are not so polite.
But he never means anything serious till he talks
    about justice right.
When he stands like an ox in the furrow—with his
    sullen set eyes on your own,
And grumbles, "This isn't fair dealing," my son, leave
    the Saxon alone.'

Rudyard Kipling, 'Norman and Saxon' (1911)

When the computer pioneer Alan Turing was sent to the USA in 1942 to help the Americans build their own code-breaking computers, he found something quite different from the eclectic and somewhat eccentric approach to code-breaking adopted by the English authorities. Instead of the peculiar mixture of mathematicians and crossword puzzlers, he found a group of lawyers.

Turing's discovery does throw into sharp relief the peculiarly English approach to problem-solving, highlighted by the code-breaking efforts in the Second World War. Around him at the secret establishment at Bletchley Park were not just mathematicians, but linguists, statisticians, puzzle creators, and strange individuals, from the future novelist Angus Wilson to the future Home Secretary Roy Jenkins and the future historian Asa Briggs, all of them in their own enclosed huts, revealing nothing to the outside world and little to each other.

There were Egyptologists, bridge players, even one expert on seaweeds and mosses who had been sent there because of a misunderstanding of the biological term 'cryptogams', and who played a critical role working out how to dry out code books damaged by seawater. The historian Hugh Trevor-Roper, who visited often, described the atmosphere as 'friendly informality verging on apparent anarchy'. One military policeman famously mistook Bletchley for a military asylum.

Turing was the archetypal English boffin, bizarrely, logically unconventional. He wore a gas mask on his bike to avoid the pollen. He
famously chained his mug to a radiator and used string to hold up
his trousers. He was often unshaven, or – even more peculiar in a
semi-military world – was to be found knitting in a corner. He was
briefly a member of the Home Guard, but got bored of it in 1942
and stopped turning up. The commander tried to frighten him with
military law, only to find that on his application form, under the
question 'Do you understand that by enrolling in the Home Guard
you place yourself liable to military law?', Turing had written 'No'.

What made Bletchley Park distinctively English was its approach
to being a boffin, the respect for peculiarity, the faith in the cross-
disciplinary fertilisation of ideas, the idea that clever people should
be free to nose around into whatever intrigued them. It was an
approach that clearly pre-dated Churchill, but which clearly exemplified his own approach.

Churchill, after all, had some hint of a boffin about himself. He
dreamed up the idea of a tank back in 1914. He was an influential
supporter of the Mulberry harbour system of floating wharves which
made it possible to offload the equipment for the D-Day armies off
the Normandy coast in 1944. It was Churchill who insisted that his
scientists – notably the physicist R. V. Jones – should carry on inves-
tigating navigation radio beams used by German bombers, when his
scientific advisors assured him that such things did not exist.

Boffins such as Robert Watson-Watt (Scottish), or Barnes Wallis
(from Derbyshire), and their successors in the development of Blue
Streak and Concorde, turned what had been a term of abuse into an
accolade. The origins of the word are unclear but it seems to have
started with a character in Charles Dickens' *Our Mutual Friend*
(1864–5) who is described as 'a very odd-looking fellow indeed'.

Perhaps the portrayal of Q in the James Bond films as a fussy civil servant was a sign that the boffin was on the way out. The boffin's great successor, the nerd, is, after all, a product of California rather than England.

In 2011, Eric Schmidt, Google chairman, named three technologies invented by English boffins:

Photography (strictly speaking, this was only Henry Fox Talbot's paper-based negatives)
Computers
Television (strictly speaking, this was invented by a Scot)

Bowler hats used to dominate the streets of the City of London in the middle of the twentieth century, like so many black tortoise domes on the heads of the financial middle classes. Unusually, they were invented in England too, the most appropriate place for something that became symbolic of a certain kind of respectable Englishness. Bowler hats were created in 1849 by Edward Coke, the younger brother of the Earl of Leicester.

This was a rare moment of achievement in the life of a man who made very few other ripples on the world. Coke became a Whig politician after a forgettable minor career in the army, and held the seat of Norfolk Western in the mid-nineteenth century, but a perusal of Hansard – the parliamentary record – reveals no contributions to debate at all. Still, give him his due, by inventing the bowler hat, Coke left his mark.

Coke ordered the first one from the London hatters Lock & Co., who sub-contracted the order to Thomas and William Bowler. It was designed by himself to protect the heads of his gamekeepers from low-hanging branches – their top hats kept getting knocked off. Oddly enough, there is even a date for the day Coke came to collect it – 17 December 1849. When he unwrapped it, he put it on the floor, and jumped on it. He went away satisfied.

This was a hat originally designed for servants. In fact, the odd thing about the bowler hat is that, after Coke, it became anything but respectable. It became synonymous with people involved with horses, and within decades it had been adopted across the American West. Outlaws found it de rigueur. Butch Cassidy wouldn't have been seen dead without his bowler hat or, as he called it, his derby. The other profession that adopted it, and for similar reasons – it didn't blow off easily – was navvies. It was British railway workers who were supposed to have introduced them to Bolivia in the 1920s, where they were widely used by local women. These were supplied to Bolivia until recently by an Italian factory.

There is a peculiar ambiguity about bowler hats. Despite their original respectability, on both sides of the Atlantic – Jack Lemmon wears a bowler hat when he reaches senior management in *The Apartment* – the most famous bowler hat of them all was the one that graced the head of Charlie Chaplin as his Little Tramp. Laurel and Hardy wore bowler hats too, perhaps to imply the same thing – hopeless aspiration.

The same peculiarly mixed messages are contained in the bowler hats worn by the tramps in Samuel Beckett's nihilistic tramps in *Waiting for Godot*. Beckett said many years later that when he started thinking about the play, the only thing he knew was that both characters wore bowler hats.

As a cure for the cold, take your toddy to bed, put one bowler hat at the foot, and drink until you see two.

Sir Robert Bruce-Lockhart (1887–1970),
spymaster, diplomat and journalist

I f Englishmen have a reputation for buttoned-up dullness, for the kind of alluring fashion sense that means they wear socks in bed, long johns and tweeds by the fire, then Byron tips the balance the other way. Byron was the model of the great English lover, his affairs passionate and numerous and involving both sexes and probably also his own half-sister, Augusta.

Byron defied the ideal for an English gent by being terrible at football and cricket (he had a club foot) – though having said that, he was in the team for the very first Eton versus Harrow cricket match at Lord's in 1805. It was at love that he really excelled, in a kind of destructive and scandalous way, leaving the wreckage behind him – scandals which eventually forced him to leave the country, probably for fear of prosecution for sodomy. Once abroad, he ended up as an enthusiastic participant in the Greek revolution against Turkish rule, where he died of fever at the age of thirty-six.

Byron managed his legendary sexual attraction despite being born with a club foot, which he unfairly blamed on his mother.

Byron was a great lover, but he was also a great hater – one of the few parliamentary defenders of the Luddites, he was also pretty ferocious towards his fellow Romantic poets. He could not stand the poetry of Coleridge, and he referred to his famous contemporary William Wordsworth as 'Turdsworth'.

In his own lifetime, there were many who regarded him as the greatest poet in the world. These days, his reputation is not quite so high. But he does represent a particular English type: one who becomes a celebrity in his own life, who disdains convention, a mild revolutionary whose own secrets hang heavy and who dies self-destructively and in exile.

Byron himself was over-romantic about most things, veering wildly between men and women, just as he veered between an abstemious diet of biscuits and white wine and great roaring gorges on meat and everything that went with it. The poet of the Victorian age, Alfred Tennyson, remembered the news of Byron's death when he was fifteen. 'Byron was dead! I thought the whole world was at an end,' he said. 'I thought everything was over and finished for everyone – that nothing else mattered. I remembered I walked out alone, and carved "Byron is dead" into the sandstone.'

> Polygamy may well be held in dread,
> Not only as a sin, but as a bore:
> Most wise men, with one moderate woman wed,
> Will scarcely find philosophy for more.
>
> *Byron,* Don Juan, *Canto VI*

There was something of Flashman about James Thomas Brudenell, Seventh Earl of Cardigan. He appears as the villain in many of George Macdonald Fraser's *Flashman* novels, but in fact Cardigan's life was stranger even than those – he was a pompous bully, a military incompetent, who narrowly avoided arrest on a technicality for fighting a duel. By an accident of history, one of the many cock-ups of the Crimean War, Cardigan was mistakenly ordered into action with his Light Brigade to charge the Russian guns head-on at the Battle of Balaclava in 1854. His connection with the incident turned him into a national hero on his return, and in particular it immortalised the woollen garments that he took to war in the Crimea.

The English have a peculiar penchant for naming everyday objects after the peculiar, usually aristocratic, individuals who originated them – the wellington boot and the sandwich spring to mind – and so it was that woollen waistcoats open at the front became known, from that day to this, as cardigans.

Within a few weeks of the rapturous reception of Lord Cardigan after he arrived back in Folkestone at the end of the war, it became clear that all was not quite as it seemed. He did seem to have led the charge, reached the guns and escaped unscathed. Then the rumours began to circulate, that he had fled the battlefield while later waves under his command were still charging, or – more likely – that he galloped back to his own lines while the charge was still progressing.

He laid a charge of criminal libel against some of his fellow officers who made the claims, though unsuccessfully, and oblivious arrogance allowed him to continue in his post as colonel-in-chief until his retirement. His arrogance as he accompanied the Prince of Wales to inspect Prussian cavalry manoeuvres in 1861 was enough to attract several challenges to duels. He died from a fall from his horse in 1868, soon after changing his mind after a lifetime resisting political reform, and speaking in favour of the Second Reform Act. This appears to have been too much for him.

Whatever the truth of Cardigan's conduct during the Battle of Balaclava, the Charge of the Light Brigade provided English culture not just with Tennyson's poem of the same name but a strange woollen peculiarity, also popular in California (Starsky and Hutch, the TV detectives, wore versions of them) which has become a symbol of staid, middle-class solidity.

There are modern cardigans, even trendy cardigans, but the basic idea remains that cardigans are what husbands wear when they lose all connection with their youth and when the last drops of sex appeal finally evaporate, and they settle down to a life of slippered respectability.

Cardigans get a bad press, but admit it – you love them!

Headline in the Guardian, *2014*

The hopelessly heroic charge of the Light Brigade against the Russian guns at the Battle of Balaclava in 1854 has gone down in history as an example of English valour. After all, it's the Russian guns seized at Sebastopol that have provided the metal for the Victoria Cross ever since, the highest military decoration in the UK awarded for extreme courage in the face of the enemy. But it ought perhaps to be better remembered as an example of one of the darker sides of English life, snobbery and incompetence.

There certainly were 'cannons to the right of them, cannons to the left of them' as Tennyson said there were in his famous poem. But there were 673 of the Light Brigade, not the gallant 600, and only fifteen per cent of them survived with horses intact after this incompetently ordered full-frontal attack on the Russian guns.

The problem was that the commander-in-chief Lord Raglan's original orders were ambiguous. Which guns were to be attacked? It was never made clear. The next problem was that the ambiguous orders then underwent minimal discussion between the three men who loathed each other: Cardigan, his immediate commander and brother-in-law Lord Lucan, and Captain Nolan, who delivered the message on a flimsy bit of paper, and who – when he was asked which guns the order referred to – replied with a wide sweep of his arm in the vague direction of the wrong ones.

As the cavalry streamed into the Valley of Death (Tennyson's phrase) Nolan veered across their path – perhaps because he realised they were heading in the wrong direction – but was killed shortly afterwards so we will never know.

Cardigan himself withdrew from the battlefield once he had reached the guns, without stopping to see what had happened to his remaining troops, because he was seething with rage against Nolan – for, as it seemed to him, trying to steal the honour of leading the brigade into action.

This combination of snobbery, mutual contempt and suspicion of intelligence, and a bizarre reliance on frontal assaults, seems to have occurred at various unfortunate junctures in English military history, and the Light Brigade were only the most spectacular victims of it. When he came to write about military incompetence, the former Royal Engineer turned psychologist Norman Dixon said that, instead of being a warning to incompetent generals in later conflicts, the valour of the charge turned out to be an encouragement for other futile frontal assaults, right up to the disastrous Battle of the Somme and beyond.

The trumpeter who sounded the charge, Trumpeter Lanfrey, made a recording of the sound in Park Lane in London in 1890, one of the earliest Edison recordings. The same recording includes one of Florence Nightingale, the great heroine of the Crimean War. 'God bless our dear old comrades of Balaclava,' she said, 'and bring them safe to shore.'

But what, My Lord, was the feeling and what the bearing of those brave men who returned to the position? Of each of these regiments there returned but a small detachment, two thirds of the men engaged having been destroyed. I think that every man who was engaged in that disastrous affair at Balaklava, and who was fortunate enough to come out of it alive, must feel that it was only by a merciful decree of Almighty Providence that he escaped from the greatest apparent certainty of death which could possibly be conceived.

Lord Cardigan's speech to the Mansion House, 1855

There was a time when the English churchyard played the kind of role that a larder or utility room does in a modern house. It was a place for keeping things that didn't really fit anywhere else. In the medieval open-field system, all the local land was divided into strips among the people who lived in a village. Trees got in the way. That meant that the yew tree, for example – the source of the wood for the English longbow – was planted in the churchyard. The local priest was also responsible for looking after those other, rather important, elements of the local economy that were held in common: the local boar and the local bull. If people wanted their cattle impregnated, they went to the churchyard – and asked the priest.

And then again, churchyards have been – at least since the sixth century – the consecrated ground that became the home of the dead. The graves of the villagers are there, as Thomas Hardy described in

'Friends Beyond' ('And the Squire, and Lady Susan, lie in Mellstock churchyard now'), in a classless gathering that also included 'Tranter Reuben'.

This provides opportunities for inscriptions, most of which are deadly dull or pious, or both, but occasionally they are fascinating or funny. Like this one said to be from Winterbourne Steepleton in Dorset:

> Here lies the body
> Of Margaret Bent
> She kicked up her heels
> And away she went.

It is this juxtaposition of life and death – the means to create new cattle and the remains of the former villagers – that gives village churchyards their peculiar power and restfulness, perhaps most of all at the traditional lychgate. This is the covered archway where the priest originally received the corpse of a parishioner for burial, just as it is the first gate that married couples go through out into the world after their wedding – which is why it is sometimes closed by local children and only opened for a fee.

Lychgates are also a traditional place for flirting, which has always been a secondary purpose for a parish churchyard, because graves were often places to be alone at night – and even in the daytime they provided opportunities. The church was where young men and women could meet perfectly respectably, eye each other up and down inside the nave, and then maybe talk as they passed out of the gate.

The same juxtaposition is there in the most famous English poem on the subject, Thomas Gray's 'Elegy written in a Country Churchyard'. Gray was a Cambridge scholar and later professor who disapproved of his fellows (he called them 'sleepy, drunken, dull, illiterate Things'). He had been haunted by the deaths of friends and relatives, and by his friend Horace Walpole's narrow escape from highwaymen, and wrote the poem as a kind of meditation after his move to Stoke Poges in Buckinghamshire. This is how he prefaced the poem to Walpole in 1750, enclosing a copy:

> As I live in a place where even the ordinary tattle of the town arrives not till it is stale, and which produces no events of its own, you will not desire any excuse from me for writing so seldom, especially as of all people living I know you are the least a friend to letters spun out of one's own brains, with all the toil and constraint that accompanies sentimental productions. I have been here at Stoke a few days (where I shall continue good part of the summer); and having put an end to a thing, whose beginnings you have seen long ago. I immediately send it you. You will, I hope, look upon it in light of a thing with an end to it; a merit that most of my writing have wanted, and are like to want, but which this epistle I am determined shall not want.

Walpole sent it to his friends, and they passed it to others, until Gray was forced to publish it himself to prevent pirate copies going into production. It is the very essence of the gentle English art of melancholy. It also includes some of the most famous phrases in the language, including 'kindred spirit' and the phrase that would eventually inspire Hardy: 'Far from the madding crowd'.

Only eight years after it was published, the young general James Wolfe recalled it as he sat quietly with his men in boats below the Heights of Abraham to take the city of Quebec from the French. Wolfe was killed in the battle, but as he waited for the first light of dawn beforehand, he recited the poem from memory.

'Gentlemen,' he said, when he reached the end. 'I would rather have written that poem than take Quebec.'

The curfew tolls the knell of parting day,
The lowing herd wind slowly o'er the lea,
The ploughman homeward plods his weary way,
And leaves the world to darkness and to me.

Now fades the glimm'ring landscape on the sight,
And all the air a solemn stillness holds,
Save where the beetle wheels his droning flight,
And drowsy tinklings lull the distant folds;

Save that from yonder ivy-mantled tow'r
The moping owl does to the moon complain
Of such, as wand'ring near her secret bow'r,
Molest her ancient solitary reign.

C rumpets are perhaps one of the greatest examples of English food – and if the Internet is to be believed they were 'invented in 1274 by Alfred the Great'. While there's absolutely no evidence of this, of course, Alfred (see Chapter 1) did have a historic link with baking cakes – having allowed some to burn during a particularly intense bout of thinking – and he had only been dead some four centuries by 1274, so you never know.

But there is no doubt that crumpets, a mixture of milk, flour, salt and yeast, and baked on a cast iron griddle in 'crumpet rings', stretch way back, long before recorded history in England. There is a reference to a *crumpit* in 1649, made of buckwheat flour, and another one in 1769, which appears to be the earliest reference with the modern spelling.

Most authorities say the Saxons invented crumpets, but it seems that there are Celtic origins before that, and not in England either – via the *krampochs* of Brittany and the *crempogs* of Wales, both of which were variations on a pancake theme.

The idea of adding in the holes and putting in more baking flour, to give crumpets the familiar spongy feel, flat on the bottom and oozing with butter on top, seems to have begun much more recently, an innovation traced to the new industrial bakers of the Midlands in the nineteenth century.

Whatever its origins, there is something extraordinary about the English crumpet, the butter melting out of its copious pores, which gives a gravitas and satisfaction to teatime – another peculiarly English convention – which no other food can quite provide. With jam, honey or Marmite, it evokes safe nursery worlds by the fire, with damp, foggy evenings outside. It evokes comfort and childhood.

Indeed, something about the dingy autumnal weather demands crumpets. They are an English food to suit a particular English mood.

To make tea crumpets Beat two eggs very well, put them to a quart of warm milk and water, and a large spoonful of barm: beat in as much fine flour as will make them rather thicker than a common batter pudding, then make your bakestone very hot, and rub it with a little butter wrapped in a clean linen cloth, then pour a large spoonful of batter upon your stone, and let it run to the size of a tea-saucer; turn it, and when you want to use them roast them very crisp, and butter them.

Elizabeth Raffald, The Experienced English Housekeeper *(1769)*

I n the 1970s, there was an upsurge in the popularity of the far right, pedalling a potent and unpleasant mixture of racism and bigotry. It was fascinating to note in articles at the time, that – despite the racist language – they still ate in their favourite Indian curry houses. However boneheaded the English may be, however disapproving of foreign influence, they still embrace Indian cuisine as their own.

The clue to this is the word curry itself, which tends to mean any hot food and was first used in England in a book title *The Forme of Cury*, which was published in the 1390s. In those days, all hot food was called 'cury' from the French word *cuire*, which meant 'cook'.

The argument is not completely straightforward because other people claim that the word comes from the Tamil word *kari*, which was originally a thin, spiced dressing served in southern India. In any case, curry as the English understand it is just hot, spicy food and that can come from anywhere across the Far East.

Indian food as eaten in England is something of an amalgam. The whole idea of curry powder, specially prepared mixtures of spices, was developed to sell to English merchants in the eighteenth century. English curry houses date back even further, to the Hindoostanee Coffee House. This was opened in London's George Street in 1810 by an East India Company captain called Sake Dean Mahomed. It went out of business a year later.

Even the dishes served in traditional Indian restaurants tend to have names that are derived from some vague original. Words like 'vindaloo' or 'korma' are just as much from England as they are from the Indian subcontinent. The whole idea of balti dishes was developed in Birmingham. Some of the traditional English–Indian food has even managed to make its way back to India.

In fact, the traditional English curry house is particularly derived from East Bengal and from Bangladesh. This is partly because of the links between East Bengal and the London Docks, which led so many people from there to stay and then settle in the East End of London – and which made London's Brick Lane into curry-house central for the nation. By the end of the twentieth century, eighty-five per cent of all Indian restaurants in the UK were Bangladeshi.

But whether they are English or Indian in origin, or some strange amalgam of the two, they are firmly embedded as a part of English culture – a reward for being a pioneering trading nation, and for all the effort spent building up a dominance in trade to the Indian subcontinent in the great days of mercantile struggle, when the English traders had to elbow aside first the Portuguese, then the French and Dutch, to control the trade routes. The result of all that effort is the curry house at the end of the road.

To make a currey the Indian way:

Take two small chickens, skin them and cut them as for a fricassee, wash them clean, and stew them in about a quart of water for about five minutes, then strain off the liquor and put the chickens in a clean dish; take three large onions, chop them small, and fry them in about two ounces of butter, then put in the chickens and fry them in about two ounces of butter, then put in the chickens and fry them together till they are brown, take a quarter of an ounce of turmerick, and a large spoonful of ginger and beaten pepper together, and a little salt to your palate and strew all these ingredients over the chickens whilst it is frying, then pour in the liquor, and let it stew about half an hour, then put in a quarter of a pint of cream and the juice of two lemons, and serve it up. The ginger, pepper, and turmerick must be beat very fine.

Hannah Glasse, The Art of Cookery Made Plain and Easy *(1747)*

It is quite impossible to generalise about the output of the Ealing Studios in the 1940s and 1950s and their impact on the way that the English understood themselves. There were historical musicals like *Champagne Charlie* and gritty police dramas like *The Blue Lamp*, and of course the famous Ealing comedies, like *The Man in the White Suit*.

It is the spirit of *Passport to Pimlico* which sums up the anarchic sense of Englishness. There is Stanley Holloway, leading his small community of Londoners, filmed next to the Imperial War Museum, declaring independence from the British state – and holding off the forces of British bureaucracy with tit-for-tat passport inspections on the Underground as it rumbles under the new border. When the official loudspeaker van descends, one of the community shouts: 'We're sick and tired of your voice in this country – now shut up!' There was the authentic voice of Englishness, as portrayed by the Ealing machine.

Passport to Pimlico was a celebration of make-do-and-mend, of community spirit in adversity, and definitely of Anglo-Saxon awkwardness. And when they finalise the negotiations to bring Pimlico back into the English fold, the heavens open and it begins to rain.

The Ealing Studios were bought originally for film-making in 1902 and films are still being made there, so that makes it the oldest continuously used studio in the world. But it was under the leadership of Michael Balcon, in the years straddling the Second World

War, when they most successfully portrayed the English to themselves – and also the Scots (*The Maggie* and *Whisky Galore!*).

But it was the comedies that particularly lodged themselves in the national psyche, often celebrations of the peculiarities of small working-class communities, with a kind of gutsy energy – full of loveable rogues who nearly get away with their crimes (*The Lavender Hill Mob* and *Kind Hearts and Coronets*).

The comedies culminated in *The Ladykillers* in 1955, in which a group of gangsters – including Alec Guinness and Peter Sellers – lodge with an old lady near King's Cross Station. Despite the recognisably English tone, it was actually written by the American screenwriter William Rose, who claimed to have dreamed the whole thing and had to write it all down when he woke up.

Stanley Holloway played in the greatest of all the comedies, *The Titfield Thunderbolt*, in which a small rural community take on the management of their local railway when it is closed by the brand new nationalised rail operator British Rail, and face down opposition from the corrupt bus operator.

The film was released in 1953 and seems to have been inspired by the screenwriter T. E. B. ('Tibby') Clarke's visit to see Tom Rolt two years before, then in the very earliest stages of rescuing the abandoned slate railway at Talyllyn, the first of the volunteer-run revived steam railways which have since become such a feature of British life.

Holloway, George Relph and John Gregson were pioneers in more ways than one. During the inquiry by the inspector from the Ministry of Transport, Gregson takes to the floor in a desperate moment and shouts at the audience: 'You realise you're condemning our village to death? Open it up to buses and lorries and what's it going to be like in five years' time? Our lanes will be concrete roads, our houses will have numbers instead of names, there'll be traffic lights and zebra crossings.'

Of course, his prophecy came true – had already come true by 1953 – but little did Clarke know that his next-door neighbour at the time was Richard Beeching, the man who ten years later would preside over the destruction of the English branch-line network.

By Jove, Holland, it's a good job we're both honest men.

Stanley Holloway in The Lavender Hill Mob, *as he realises how it might be possible to steal a consignment of gold*

Top ten Ealing comedies:

Champagne Charlie
Hue and Cry
Kind Hearts and Coronets
Passport to Pimlico
The Ladykillers
The Lavender Hill Mob
The Maggie
The Man in the White Suit
The Titfield Thunderbolt
Whisky Galore!

At the end of the very best full-length Laurel and Hardy film, *Way Out West,* Oliver Hardy proclaims that he is going back to the South. 'Oh for a slice of possum and yam,' he says.

Stan Laurel, who – as everyone knows – was English, says that he is going back to the south too.

'The south of where, sir?' demands his friend.

'The south of London,' says Stan. 'Good old fish and chips.'

Perhaps American audiences couldn't have been expected to know Ulverston in Cumbria where Laurel actually hailed from. But it so happens that the decade of *Way Out West* marked the high point in the rise of the English fish and chip shop. There were 35,000 of them in the British Isles in 1929. That figure has sunk considerably since, but they still use a tenth of all the potatoes eaten in the nation.

Fish and chips had become our national dish, certainly for the working classes, and although its origins may be lost in the mists of time, these particular mists were not that long ago. Charles Dickens described fried-fish shops in *Oliver Twist* in 1838, when the fish came with baked potatoes or bread. Sometime in the 1860s, fish and chips first emerged as a classic combination. One possible originator was the Jewish immigrant Joseph Malinin from London's East End, who first wrapped up fish and potatoes in old newspaper – a practice that carried on into the 1980s. Another was the Lancashire shopkeeper John Lees, working out of Mossley Market in Greater Manchester.

The modern combination of newspaper, greasy chips, vinegar,

pickled eggs, cockles and mussels seems to have emerged from various different influences at once: the chips probably from Belgium, the fried fish brought by Jewish immigrants from Spain and Portugal and spread by Italian immigrant families to England in the final decades of the nineteenth century. In *The Road to Wigan Pier* (1937) George Orwell suggested that fish and chips might have averted revolution – the cheapness and comfort, especially on a dank English evening, does certainly have an extraordinary power to cheer you up.

Wartime civilians in both world wars seemed to sense the defence implications of fish and chips, the 'good companions' as Winston Churchill described them. War Cabinets went to enormous lengths to make sure they were never rationed. By then, they already felt a little patriotic.

Oldest fish and chip shop in the world:
Yeadon near Leeds (1865)

The American novelist Gore Vidal was so obsessed with the forgetfulness of his fellow countrymen that he renamed the nation Amnesia. Something similar afflicts the English. It isn't that their memories are faulty, it is just that they assume that what was true recently was always true. It is a strange English kind of conservatism.

The English like to think that all their most beloved institutions date back sometime to the arrival of Noah on Mount Ararat, when actually most of them seem to have started around 1859–64. Charles Darwin's theory of evolution, John Lewis department store, the London Underground, the Football Association, lawn tennis, you name it.

Another beloved institution, born in 1862, was the Flying Scotsman, or as it was actually known back then, the Special Scotch Express. Two expresses started simultaneously that year from London King's

Cross and Edinburgh Waverley. They journey took ten hours, with a half-hour lunch in York.

The real drama of the Flying Scotsman came in two explosions of competitive Races to the North, in August 1888 and August 1895 when – although the directors never admitted that there was a race – the rival managers of the west and east coast main lines struggled for the title of the fastest service. It began in 1888 when the London and North Western Railway announced at the last minute that they were re-timing the arrival of their Day Scotch Express by one hour. Crowds greeted the trains at Euston and King's Cross when they set off and cheered the trains at Carlisle, even in the middle of the night. Reporters accompanied the trip as the services steamed through the night for Edinburgh and on to Aberdeen.

Two things conspired to end the competition. The first was that arriving in Aberdeen at half-past four in the morning was virtually useless for everybody, and there was also a derailment at speed in 1896. The rival companies agreed to cool it.

When the LNER Flying Scotsman train service began under that name in 1927, it was a non-stop service, and there was a corridor so that a new shift of drivers and firemen could take over without stopping at a station. Even then, their rivals at the London, Midland and Scottish Railway put on a new non-stop train to Glasgow leaving at the same time. The actual *Flying Scotsman* locomotive had tested out the feasibility of this service back in 1924 and managed to get up to a top speed of 100 mph for the first time.

They were heady days, with a restaurant car and a barber on board for the customers. But they are gone, and since 1958 the Flying Scotsman Service has been hauled by a diesel. Anyone who wants to get from London to Edinburgh fast nowadays tends to fly. These days, the train advertised as the Flying Scotsman stops at York and

Newcastle and travels at an average speed of just below 100 mph. It isn't quite the same.

When the English think of the Flying Scotsman service today, they tend to think of three things. The first is the idea of the journey, the string luggage shelves above the heads of the passengers, the mirrors behind the chairs in the compartments, the porters in black and making your away through the steam on the platform from the buffet, after tea and toast. The second is the *Night Mail* film by the Post Office, with its poem by W. H. Auden and music by Benjamin Britten. We also think of the 1923 locomotive (No. 4472), still in existence, and still roving across the rail network of the nation.

For a century it has been with us. Out on the great fens, across the Plain of York, in the hill villages of the North-East and in the Border farms, people have set their clocks by it, down the long years.

C. Hamilton Ellis, describing the endurance of the Flying Scotsman, 1968

There never was an English composer more able to conjure up a hummable tune than Arthur Sullivan. There is a class of English intellectual superiority that peers down its nose at Gilbert and Sullivan operettas, as if they fail to rise to the level you expect of Glyndebourne or the Royal Opera House, where they are very rarely if ever played ('What, never? Well, hardly ever!').

But if the great age of tunes petered out in the 1960s, it began in the 1860s, and Sullivan – the son of a bandmaster who managed to master every instrument in the band by the age of eight – was at the very forefront. It wasn't just the melodies of 'Poor Wandering One' or 'The Sun Whose Rays', it was great Victorian classics like 'The Lost Chord' and hymns too. He adapted the music for the hymn with the best tune of all: 'It Came Upon a Midnight Clear'.

Though he chafed at the ridiculous plots he composed to, and the time they took – he longed to write grand opera – it was Sullivan whose music keeps Gilbert's words afloat well over a century later.

William Schwenck Gilbert was certainly not the junior partner. He was an innovative and inventive man of the theatre, with a clear view of what his productions should look like, which he drove through with a single-minded, grumpy determination.

Gilbert's words and comic sense certainly stand the test of time – his patter songs like 'I've got it on my list' and 'The Modern Major-General' still resonate now. His brilliant lampoons of English government live on in *The Mikado* (though the English establishment, being what it is, suppressed a production of *The Mikado* in honour of the state visit of the Japanese prince in 1907 in case it gave offence).

Gilbert was an ill-tempered tyrant with a hugely generous streak, and his argument about the costs of a carpet nearly undermined the partnership with Sullivan and the D'Oyly Carte Opera Company completely. It was a series of flops in the 1890s that finally managed that. The public eventually outgrew Gilbert and Sullivan, the scenery of the various D'Oyly Carte touring companies began to fall apart, and it took Jonathan Miller's brilliant reimagining of *The Mikado* at the English National Opera in 1987 – and Mike Leigh's portrayal in the film *Topsy-Turvy* in 1999 – to bring Gilbert and Sullivan back into fashion.

Richard D'Oyly Carte and his wife Helen were a key element of the Gilbert and Sullivan partnership. They formed the agreement after D'Oyly Carte's previous business partners lost their heads during the production of *HMS Pinafore*, and sent thugs on stage to seize the scenery.

But it was Sullivan's music that ensured the brilliant, yet very peculiar, contemporary satire became a lasting contribution to English culture – the juxtaposition of fairies and the House of Lords in *Iolante*, or the presiding judge marrying the key witness in *Trial by Jury*, might not have been achievable by every composer. It was also Sullivan's determination that he needed emotion in order to compose effectively which forced Gilbert – as far as Gilbert could ever be forced – into providing plots which might last.

The collaboration began with *Thespis* in 1871, the music and lyrics of which have since been lost, right through to the disastrous *Grand Duke* in 1896.

Sullivan never married and carried on a series of affairs, including with the American socialite Fanny Reynolds. He had previously carried on secret affairs simultaneously with two sisters, the daughters of the engineer John Scott Russell. Like many English gentlemen, he very much enjoyed life in Paris, loved gambling, and had a knack for some of the great English sports – and not others. 'I have seen some bad lawn-tennis players in my time,' said his leading man George Grossmith, 'but I never saw anyone so bad as Arthur Sullivan.'

Sullivan suffered recurrent ill health, and his kidney disease forced him to conduct sitting down. He died aged only fifty-eight with his opera *The Emerald Isle* still unfinished on his desk. Gilbert lived until 1911 when he dived into his own garden pond to rescue girls he believed were drowning (they were just larking about) and the sudden cold gave him a heart attack. It was somehow a thoroughly Gilbertian ending.

Their influence can be felt in the lyrics of P. G. Wodehouse in his Hollywood screenwriting days, right through to the satire of Tom Lehrer. Sullivan's songs formed the basis of the great tradition of hummable tunesmiths, including George Gershwin, Richard Rodgers and maybe even Andrew Lloyd Webber. They launched the humorous career of Grossmith too, author of *The Diary of a Nobody*. In fact the Gilbert tradition of English satire is one which punctures the airs of the pompous and the fatuous, and continues to this day as a distinctive pillar of English life.

In enterprise of martial kind,
When there was any fighting,
He led his regiment from behind
(He found it less exciting).
But when away his regiment ran,
His place was at the fore, O –
That celebrated,
Cultivated,
Underrated
Noble man,
The Duke of Plaza-Toro!

W. S. *Gilbert,* The Gondoliers *(1889)*

The English cling to their history, and not just the nice bits. They cling obsessively to their festivals commemorating bloody defeats or capitulations (see Chapter 33). The idea of creating a kind of effigy of a man, putting him on top of a bonfire every year and letting off fireworks to celebrate his demise, is one of the most peculiar, not to say embarrassing, of our national habits.

Fawkes was born in York in 1570 and became a Catholic under the influence of his stepfather. Like so many religious obsessives, he went abroad to fight for the cause – fighting Dutch Protestants on behalf of Spanish Catholics in the Low Countries, and travelling to Spain to try to get support for some kind of English revolution. He failed, but ran into his fellow plotter Thomas Wintour, who in turn introduced him to Robert Catesby, and so the plot to assassinate James I developed, link by link.

Fawkes was a big man with a bushy red beard and moustache. He was recommended by a Jesuit friend of his as 'pleasant of approach and cheerful of manner, opposed to quarrels and strife . . . loyal to his friends'.

The plotters met for the first time in May 1604 in a pub called the Duck and Drake on the Strand in London. The plan was to blow up Parliament along with the king at the state opening, and to replace him with his daughter Elizabeth. There would be a simultaneous uprising in the Midlands. In the end, the business of planting the gunpowder couldn't have been easier. They simply rented the under-croft beneath the House of Lords.

What gave them away were the qualms that terrorists tend to have when they are civilised people. An anonymous letter was sent to the Catholic Lord Monteagle, urging him to stay away. He showed it to the king, the undercroft was searched and Fawkes was discovered, along with thirty-six barrels of gunpowder, designed – according to the conspirators – 'to blow you Scotch beggars back to your native mountains'.

He was tortured until he revealed the names of his conspirators. All were found guilty in the Lords, watched secretly by the king and his family. Fawkes was the last to die in Old Palace Yard, managing to fling himself off the scaffold and break his neck before the agonies of being hanged, drawn and quartered.

King James himself suggested that their 'joyful deliverance' ought to be celebrated with bonfires every year on 5 November and the tradition soon caught on. Fireworks began about half a century later and they have continued ever since. Although the dangers of fireworks have muted the general mayhem in recent years, Bonfire Night – and the smell of burned cardboard, wet sparklers or the traditional ginger parkin – remains an essential part of English childhood.

William Harrison Ainsworth's 1841 novel *Guy Fawkes* began the rehabilitation of Fawkes as a kind of anti-hero. He is a sympathetic character in the book and, in the century and a half that followed, Guy Fawkes has developed less as a villain and more as a kind of symbol of defiance against vested interests. This may be peculiar for a man who was a terrorist, after all, committed to the victory of another nation with which England was at war; but in the end, despite all the drawing and quartering, the English are a forgiving lot. It just takes them a few centuries to discover that Fawkes was a heroic character, and to don his masks from the film *V for Vendetta* to demonstrate outside Parliament.

Remember, remember the Fifth of November,
The Gunpowder Treason and Plot,
I know of no reason
Why the Gunpowder Treason
Should ever be forgot.
Guy Fawkes, Guy Fawkes, t'was his intent
To blow up the King and Parli'ment.
Three-score barrels of powder below
To prove old England's overthrow;
By God's providence he was catch'd
With a dark lantern and burning match.
Holla boys, holla boys, let the bells ring.
Holloa boys, holloa boys, God save the King!
And what should we do with him? Burn him!

Traditional rhyme for 5 November

I s there anything that remains English about Harrods department store? It has been in foreign ownership since 1985. Most of its shoppers are foreign. The former owner, Mohammed al Fayed, had peculiarities that included a dress code that meant occasionally having customers thrown out on the grounds that they were not wearing the correct clothing (thoroughly un-English).

There are two reasons for including Harrods in this book, in spite of everything. The first is its origins as a draper's shop founded by Charles Henry Harrod in 1824, in Bermondsey Street in the poverty-stricken London borough of Southwark. By the 1840s, it was a grocer in Islington and then in Stepney in the East End. By the 1850s, it was a small shop on its present site in the Brompton Road, and was built up into the retailing monster that it became by the next generation, in the form of Charles Digby Harrod.

For some reason, it is so often the second generation which makes the innovative breakthrough in English retailing. It was not Michael Marks but his son Simon who turned Marks & Spencer into the bastion of the English middle classes, selling a quarter of all socks bought in the nation. It was not the cantankerous John Lewis but his son Spedan who turned the store chain that still bears his name into the pioneer of mutualism. Harrods was no exception.

That is the first reason, and don't let us forget also that the Brompton Road site turned into one of the most valuable strips of real estate in the world, owned by the legacees of a salt merchant called Henry Smith who left the proceeds in perpetuity to the victims of Turkish slavers.

The second reason is that England more or less invented the department store. It is true that there is a reasonable challenge from Paris in the shape of Le Bon Marché, but the full flavour of a multi-department store was really the brainchild of William Whiteley, who launched his monument to Victorian consumerism in 1863 in Paddington, followed shortly afterwards by John Lewis the next year, who borrowed money from his sister to allow him to do so, and scraped all the plaster off the walls to give him more room to sell. Both represented an English revolution in retailing – it meant turning away from actively trying to persuade or cajole customers into buying things they didn't want, to encouraging them to trust.

The department-store idea also took some time to bed down, but in the end it was less trouble for Mr Pooter and the other inhabitants of the new London suburbs to order all their furniture from Whiteleys or Harrods, and have it driven round, than to be snubbed by snobbish shop assistants or sneered at for not knowing precisely what they wanted.

This is a brief explanation about how Harrods became the worldwide brand it is today, priding itself on selling everything, as it used to say, 'from a pin to an elephant'. It was Harrods which first introduced an escalator in 1898, a fearsome thing, and offered customers a glass of brandy at the top to revive them once they had risked the journey.

Still, there is no doubt that the traditional, restrained white Christmas lights still warm the heart, and there remains something spectacular about its food hall, which is perhaps why it is sometimes visited by up to 300,000 people a day.

Harrods' peculiarities:

Most famous purchase: The original Winnie-the-Pooh (1921)
Strangest purchase: A live alligator bought by Noël Coward (1951)

I t is one of those tunes that were instantly recognisable a generation ago, but now – perhaps because of an ironic distaste for bombast – have rather gone out of fashion. 'Heart of Oak' was well known as the official march of the Royal Navy, and supported a sense that oak trees and the wooden walls of England (see Chapter 42) were somehow the quintessence of the nation. In fact, it is also the official march of the Royal Canadian Navy and the Royal New Zealand Navy. The Royal Australian Navy dropped it for something more appropriate.

The words were written by the great English actor David Garrick (1717–79) and sung for the first time in 1760. The year is significant because the 'wonderful year' referred to in the first verse was 1759, the year of a string of military and naval victories, including James Wolfe's successful attempt to take Quebec (see Chapter 59) – 1759 was a kind of military version of the 2012 Olympics, when everything went rather better than expected, an unusual experience for the English.

There may be another reason 'Heart of Oak' has gone out of fashion. The English have entered one of those occasional periods when they no longer see themselves as a primarily naval nation. The photographs of warships which used to grace the front pages of our newspapers have given way to photographs of soldiers. We have become a military nation instead.

This may be a shift in the soul of the English. It may just be a temporary blip. But military nations believe in discipline and central-ised rigour and immediate obedience. Naval nations tend to be more relaxed and to believe in the flexibility and humour and individualism of a command somewhere out on the great oceans.

We will see. In the meantime, 'Heart of Oak' has been shoved rather under the carpet.

> Come, cheer up, my lads, 'tis to glory we steer,
> To add something new to this wonderful year;
> To honour we call, you as freemen not slaves,
> For who are so free as the sons of the waves?
>
> Heart of Oak are our ships,
> Jolly Tars are our men,
> We always are ready: Steady, boys, Steady!
> We'll fight and we'll conquer again and again.

The first census in England was during the Napoleonic Wars, but it was not the first nation in the world to count its population: that was Sweden. Parliament rejected the idea in 1752, on the grounds that it was an intolerable interference in people's privacy.

The man behind the plan was the former secretary of the Prince of Wales and son of the Archbishop of Canterbury, Thomas Potter, MP for St Germans – 'a man of more than middling abilities', according to *Gentleman's Magazine*, 'and somewhat conceited of his own parts'. He was defeated almost single-handedly by York MP William Thornton, who was the only MP voting against in the first vote, but by the time the legislation reached the House of Lords, he had so stoked up the opposition that they threw it out.

'Can it be pretended, that by the knowledge of our number, or our wealth, either can be increased?' Thornton asked fellow MPs. 'And what purpose will it answer to know where the kingdom is crowded, and where it is thin, except we are to be driven from place to place as graziers do their cattle? If this be intended, let them brand us at once; but while they treat us like oxen and sheep, let them not insult us with the name of men.'

You don't have to agree with Thornton to admire his courage, his boneheaded English individualism, and his determination to resist the rise of the technocrats.

The English have always regarded themselves as unbiddable. They have harboured a suspicion, both about the Napoleonic tyranny of continental Europe – buttressed perhaps by a Protestant nervousness about the tyranny of the pope (Brussels and Rome have played similar roles in the minds of the English at different periods of their history) – and about the slavish obedience of the Americans, with their jaywalking fines and perfect municipal grass. The English might complain about the resulting disorder back home, but they prefer it to the alternative. They complain that their trains are late, but have never (so far) been tempted by the apparent efficiency of totalitarianism.

There is no doubt that the result is a muddle. No written constitution. No coherent legal codes. No coherent government either: English laws and policies are the sum total of every fudge back through time. But there is something rather wonderful, as well as infuriating, about the ramshackle business of English administration, with its amateur magistrates and its unarmed police (well, usually). It is the product of English individualism, and none the worse for that.

In this age, the mere example of non-conformity, the mere refusal to bend the knee to custom, is itself a service. Precisely because the tyranny of opinion is such as to make eccentricity a reproach, it is desirable, in order to break through that tyranny, that people should be eccentric. Eccentricity has always abounded when and where strength of character has abounded; and the amount of eccentricity in a society has generally been proportional to the amount of genius, mental vigour, and moral courage which it contained. That so few now dare to be eccentric, marks the chief danger of the time.

John Stuart Mill, On Liberty *(1859)*

What is it about the north-east region of England? Yes it provided us with the Venerable Bede, the Lindisfarne Gospels, the Geordie accent and much else besides; but it has also been the source of England's great troublemakers, and as such has shaped the culture of England around it.

The Pilgrimage of Grace is generally supposed to have started with the failure of the Lincolnshire rebellion in October 1536, and to have emerged in Yorkshire under the leadership of a London barrister from Richmondshire called Robert Aske. Enraged by the behaviour of Henry VIII, as well he might have been, and suspicious of the new religion being foisted on them – and particularly about the privatisation of the welfare structures (basically what the dissolution of the monasteries amounted to) – they took over York Minster and drove the new tenants out of the monasteries.

As many as 40,000 people marched with Aske to Selby to negotiate with the dukes, arriving from all over the north and carrying with them the supposedly miraculous five-yard banner of St Cuthbert, brought by the Durham contingent. They were all given a royal pardon and a promise that the next dissolution would wait until Parliament had met in York. Then, trustingly, Aske dismissed his followers. He ended up hanged in a cage in London, and other leaders were hanged and beheaded, or hanged, drawn and quartered.

No such punishment was meted out to the Jarrow marchers, 200 of whom set off precisely four centuries after Aske in October 1936, carrying a petition signed by 11,000 people, enraged by the closure and dissolution of their local shipbuilding company, by seventy-two per cent local unemployment, and by the closure of one of only two grocery shops. There were no beheadings when they reached London a month and nearly 300 miles later, but they were snubbed by the prime minister Stanley Baldwin and given £1 each to get home again.

As in the Pilgrimage of Grace, the marchers – who called themselves the Jarrow Crusade – were blessed by the Bishop of Jarrow before they left. Halfway down, they were attacked by the Bishop of Durham as purveyors of 'revolutionary mob tactics'. In 1536, a previous Bishop of Durham had been forced to escape from his castle by a mob which had arrived to try to persuade him to lead the rebellion. In both cases, the prospect of the marchers arriving in London filled the authorities with apprehension. In 1936, the Special Branch gave the Cabinet a briefing which suggested that 'selected journalists . . . be interviewed and given material for exposing the origin, motive and uselessness of the march'.

A revealing picture now hangs at the Geffrye Museum in London of a languid young couple at the window of a smart house in central London, looking down at the burning torches of the marchers as they arrived. There is some interest, but not much. It is an evocative portrait of the strange peculiarities of the English class system.

It was the same to-day all along the road from Ripon. The villagers of Ripley and Killinghall rushed to their doors to see the marchers pass; motorists waved as they went by; one shouted, 'How are you sticking it?' and a woman cried, 'Hello, Geordies.' And the 'Geordies' themselves were in great form, so that every moment I expected the band to change from 'Annie Laurie' and 'Swanee River' to 'Cheer, Boys, Cheer'. Contributions to the 'kitty' fell in as we went; here it was a pound there it was a penny, the penny specifically being the offering of an ecstatic little girl who ran across the road to meet us as if no one less than Bonnie Prince Charlie was at our head.

The Guardian, *13 October 1936*

The Proms were created by Robert Newman, the impresario and manager of the Queen's Hall, opposite the building that is now Broadcasting House in London. In August 1895, the young conductor Henry Wood launched the series under Newman's direction.

Newman's original idea for the Proms was that they should lure the middlebrow into new experiences in music. He was aware that the idea had been tried before in Covent Garden, but had only really worked at the hands of a romantic figure like the French conductor Louis-Antoine Jullien. Henry Wood was the proposed solution and Newman took him out to lunch at Pagani's restaurant next to the old Queen's Hall. The money needed came from a music lover, a surgeon from Upper Wimpole Street, Dr George Cathcart, who funded the experiment on condition it would include Wagner.

They were promoted originally as Robert Newman's Promenade Concerts. When they opened on 10 August 1895, they were due to last for ten weeks, sixty performances, with admission of only one shilling and with another big idea – discounts for season tickets. They were a great success, but always controversial. Newman himself went bankrupt. His successor was forced out during the First World War because of his German name, and disputes about broadcasting with its new promoters (Chappell & Co.) beset the Proms during the 1920s. The saviour of the Proms was undoubtedly the BBC, which came to the rescue in 1927 and never let go, even when the venue was moved to Bedford to avoid the doodlebug raids.

The creator of the peculiar English institution known as the Last Night of the Proms was the televisual conductor Sir Malcolm Sargent, a showman who took the Proms into the television age and out of the slightly prim control of the BBC.

It was Sargent who encouraged promenaders to take a more active part, and who tolerated the banners, balloons and funny hats, and it was Sargent who set the traditional programme of the Last Night, with Wood's 'Fantasia on British Sea Songs' and Elgar's 'Pomp and Circumstance March No. 1', which first appeared on the programme to celebrate the end of the Second World War at the 1945 season. It was also Sargent who dragged himself up from his deathbed in September 1967 to be with the promenanders on the Last Night for the final time.

He did all this in the teeth of opposition from the establishment, who deeply disapproved of the antics of the crowd. 'A music-hall rabble,' said Lady Jessie Wood (Sir Henry's widow) in 1947. 'A frightening emotional orgy,' said the controller of the BBC's Light Programme. 'For the first time, I realised the full extent of the dangers that attend the popularising of music,' he wrote in 1950. 'Plato knew what he was doing when he proposed to banish music and poetry from his republic.'

But the Last Night became known around the world, and every year from 1947 – when television cameras first appeared – the paraphernalia and bacchanalia increased. In 1952, a firework smuggled in for Tchiakovsky's '1812 Overture' went off early. Sargent also had to give a pep talk to the audience about the dangers of throwing coins.

But there is something heroic about the Last Night, a wild concert with an ironic edge to it, celebrating some of the bravado of being English.

Traditional Last Night programme:

Edward Elgar: 'Pomp and Circumstance March No. 1' (including 'Land of Hope and Glory')

Henry Wood: 'Fantasia on British Sea Songs' (including 'Rule, Britannia')

Hubert Parry: 'Jerusalem'

UNDERGROUND

I f London is a nation of itself, cut off from its surroundings by the great sweeping waves of the M25, then the London Underground is a world within a world. It has its own design, its own atmosphere and people behave differently down there. Perhaps they respond to the light roar of a train approaching a packed platform, or the dark dusty swirl of old newspapers as the breeze of a distant train ruffles the hairs on the back of the mice down on the track. Perhaps their own underground comes out.

The Underground itself goes back to the year 1863. The early Tube had gaslit carriages hauled by steam locomotives. The Metropolitan Railway soon teamed up with the District Railway to create the Circle Line, finished in 1884. There are now 270 stations, some of them emphatically above ground, and it is always a surprise how new the rest is. The Bakerloo and Piccadilly lines opened in 1906, and in decaying darkness rest many of the forgotten stations, their platforms boarded up, their empty lines the preserve of the rats and yeti (Dr Who) – Down Street, Aldwych, Trafalgar Square – a strange shadowy world that remains half in and half out of reality.

What really created the Underground that we know today was a joint marketing effort in the early years of the twentieth century, using the term 'Underground' for the first time in that context – and the decision to electrify the lines at the same time. The shadowy elements, the sense of otherness, is the result of the efforts of three men.

The first was Frank Pick, a solicitor who rose to be managing director of the Underground in 1928 and ruled London Transport until 1940. Pick was an admirer of William Morris – he used green ink in his honour – and who believed like Morris in the role of design in civilisation.

Pick set out to put this thought into action in the Underground, with a strong sense of design. He used the original roundel, which is so distinctive, commissioned the latest art-deco architecture for many stations. He was also a great commissioner of poster art, with some of the most distinctive, colourful mid-century evocations of the English countryside the product of his chequebook, advertising his Green Line buses, snaking out into the rural areas. His posters advertising the suburbs evoked the emerging Metroland before the First World War. In fact, it was his standardised advertising sizes that first drew him to the attention of his superiors.

It was Pick who commissioned the calligrapher Edward Johnston to design the very distinctive typeface that has been used by the Underground ever since. Pick's fanatical attention to detail saw him wandering his stations late at night, moving ticket machines a few inches to the right or left.

But it wasn't Pick who designed the distinctive topographical Tube map. That was Harry Beck, who was inspired to draw the map in full colour when he was working on electrical diagrams. He sent it to Pick in 1931. Pick forwarded it to his publicity department who rejected it, because it didn't show the distances between stations.

Beck kept pushing and they tested it out in 1932 and the public liked it. Beck's name used to go on the bottom and they paid him, on a freelance basis, to update the map. That was until 1960 when, to his horror, Beck found his name had been removed and somebody else had added the route of the new Victoria Line.

Legal action followed and Beck kept on updating the map and submitting his designs until he gave up, with a sense of betrayal. He died in 1974 but, in 1997, the Underground had a change of heart and now his name is back on the map again. Because he worked on the map as a London Transport employee (though in his spare time), it is not clear whether he was ever actually paid for the original.

The third individual responsible for the atmosphere of the Underground has to be the poet and conservationist John Betjeman, with his evocation of Metroland and the days when trains were 'rumbling under blackened girders'.

A thing may be right and beautiful and true without being lovable, though a thing cannot be lovable without being also in itself right and beautiful and true. Love is the harmony which such a thing awakes in the emotions; it is the harmony of what it feels to be. It adds the heart, as we call it, to the conscience, the sense, and the mind, to make the four great organs of being.

Frank Pick

Underground lines:

Metropolitan Line 1863
Hammersmith & City Line 1864
District Line 1868
Circle Line 1871
Northern Line 1890
Waterloo & City Line 1898
Central Line 1900
Bakerloo Line 1906
Piccadilly Line 1906
Victoria Line 1968
Jubilee Line 1979

There are those who are a little sceptical of the whole idea of meat pies. They say that, if the manufacturer of the pies doesn't know what kind of animal gave rise to the meat, then maybe the pies should be treated as slightly dodgy.

I'm sure they are right to be nervous, but nevertheless, in flagrant disregard for the origins of the meat, English meat pies have still fuelled many a cold afternoon on the football terraces, as well as evenings working late at the factory. English lunchboxes have been graced by a meat pie for centuries.

Why this indeterminate meat? Why not just say beef or ham or chicken pie? Well, the answer appears to lie in the medieval period, when the first of our ancestors gave us the meat pie – beginning as fast food for the poorer inhabitants of medieval cities.

In London, by the docks, in the twelfth century, there emerged the phenomenon of the cookshop. It was a place where, if you had no cooking facilities yourself, you could take your joint – or whatever meat you happened to have purloined that day – and they would cook it for you. What they did was wrap it in pastry, put it in the bread oven for fifteen minutes, and out it would come. And *voilà*! A meat pie.

The pies were also sold by hawkers in the streets, in baskets covered with a muslin cloth, the beginning of the famous 'pieman'. *Piers Plowman*, creation of William Langland in the fourteenth century, remembers the street cries like this: 'Hot pies, hot good piglets and geese, go dine, go!'

By that stage of history, the main source of meat pies was in Eastcheap. The problem with cookshops was they tended just to chuck the bones and unusable bits out into the street and were therefore a public nuisance, so they tended to be moved along as the centuries went by. They were also notoriously dodgy even then. A ruling in 1301 forbade the cookshops from buying meat any more than a day old in the summer months. You could hide no end of diseased stuff in a pie.

By Tudor and Stuart times, the pie makers became more special-ised – pork pies from the north, veal and ham pies from the Midlands, steak and kidney, eel and chicken pies from the Lake District. In 1660, Samuel Pepys upbraided his wife for cooking her pies for too long in her brand-new oven, comforting himself that she'll know 'how to do better another time'.

Even so, pies remained something of a fare for poorer English people, or for those having a night on the town, when they could buy from the piemen or, after 1850s or so, from the pie shops. The piemen used to avoid complete bankruptcy by going round the pubs and offering to toss a coin with the customers for a pie. If the customers lost, they had to pay a penny; if they won, they got the pie for free – which, often enough, they would then use to throw at other customers.

It wasn't quite the sad end for the great English institution of meat pies though. In the end, they are rather a good way of keeping meat for longer. They are convenient when you are travelling or away from home. They are comforting when you bite into them and the juices and steam come out. And they do after all owe part of their inspiration to the great Tudor pies, many feet across, cooked with porpoise or elk for up to eight hours.

She made her living by selling pies,
Her meat pies were a treat,
Chock full of meat and such a size
'Cos she was getting the meat from—

Mr Sweeney Todd, the Barber.
Ba Goom, he were better than a play
Sweeney Todd, the Barber
'I'll polish them off!' he used to say.

R. P. Weston, 'Sweeney Todd'

There is something about the English which prefers things to be a little broken, unprepossing, and worn by the passage of time. It is more than the polite English preference for old things, which is a kind of English snobbery. 'He had to buy all his furniture,' said the Conservative politician Michael Jopling about Michael Heseltine, dismissively (as quoted by Alan Clark in his *Diaries*) – it is the kind of snobbery which is deeply suspicious of anything too shiny and packaged. It results in the enthusiastic commissioning of Roman or medieval ruins in country parks, and in the traditional English preference for elegies, laments and fatal departures.

The English were supposed for many centuries to be prone to melancholia, mainly because of their climate but also because beef was supposed to interfere with the digestion. That may not be the reason, but you can hear the clear note of nostalgia in Chaucer and *Hamlet*, in Gray's 'Elegy' right back to Malory's *Le Morte d'Arthur* – there is a clue there: why write the whole Arthurian legend in terms of death and loss? Then, up almost to the present generation, there was George Orwell meditating on the fate of his country village in *Coming Up for Air* (1939).

There does also seem to be a link here with the Gothic fascination with madness and insanity. 'It is worth attention that the English have more songs and ballads on the subject of madness than any of their neighbours,' wrote Bishop Thomas Percy in his *Reliques of Ancient English Poetry* (1765). There is the English attitude in a nutshell. Not only is life 'a tale told by an idiot, signifying nothing', as Shakespeare put it – but to make matters worse, upstairs in the attic is our mad wife.

The writer Peter Ackroyd talks about the English landscape, the rolling, winding roads, and the stories of generation after generation, as the basis of this sense of heaviness. He conjures up a huge empty England, as it was in the days of the invaders – with little homesteads along the South Downs and a few crumbling Roman roads, and the great impenetrable forest to the north. There was the roots of English melancholy: it is ancient, and somewhat lonely out there.

> But here in London streets I ken
> No such helpmates, only men;
> And these are not in plight to bear,
> If they would, another's care.
> They have enough as 'tis: I see
> In many an eye that measures me
> The mortal sickness of a mind
> Too unhappy to be kind.
> Undone with misery, all they can
> Is to hate their fellow man;
> And till they drop they needs must still
> Look at you and wish you ill.

A. E. Housman, 'A Shropshire Lad' XLI (1896)

The English have a habit of calling their most ancient institutions 'new' – as in New College, Oxford, which was in fact established in 1379 – and using the word 'old' to indicate something traditional. This doesn't entirely explain why there are two famous sports venues called Old Trafford, only half a mile from each other, on the outskirts of Manchester. But it is perhaps an acknowledgement that there is something older here than either football or cricket – the land involved used to belong to the old Trafford family, stretching back before the Norman Conquest.

So let's hear it, not so much for Matt Busby or Bobby Charlton or even Shane Warne, but for Radolphus de Trafford who died in 1050 (in the reign of the former patron saint of England, Edward the Confessor) – the lineal forefather of them all.

As far as sports grounds are concerned – and we are talking about hallowed ground here – the oldest of the Old Traffords is undoubtedly the cricket ground, home of Lancashire County Cricket Club, built in 1857 on the meadows belonging to the de Trafford estate. The ground was originally only accessible via a winding footpath from the railway station. The crowds began to flock there to see W. G. Grace in the 1870s. When the Ashes Test match between England and Australia was held there in 1884, Old Trafford's future was assured. It was also the scene in 1956 when Jim Laker managed to take nineteen wickets for just ninety runs, an achievement that has never been bettered.

Wander about 800 yards and there is the other Old Trafford, the football ground and home of Manchester United, probably the most famous football team in the world.

Manchester United used to be known as Newton Heath and suffered from a series of disastrous grounds, either on marshland or on gravel. Their final temporary stadium was in Bank Street, where fumes from the local factory cast an annoying pall over the experience of spectators. New owner John Henry Davies chose the site for their new stadium, designed it to take crowds of 100,000 and managed to get it open by 1910. The first game held was against Liverpool (Manchester United lost). It has been in use ever since – with a brief hiatus in the 1940s when it was damaged by German bombs. The stadium never quite managed to hold 100,000 fans as intended – the biggest crowd they ever managed was in March 1939 with the FA Cup semi-final between Grimsby and Wolverhampton Wanderers.

Old Trafford has hosted rugby games, Olympics events and a great many other fixtures. The international following for Manchester United began to grow in the 1950s, and under the leadership of Alex Ferguson (manager 1986–2013), Old Trafford has gained a mystique that no amount of money from American sports magnates can quite dispel.

In many ways, Old Trafford has as good a claim as anywhere else to be the spiritual home of English football. Having said that, the only part of the original 1910 stadium to survive is the old players' tunnel – and that isn't used any more.

Biggest crowds at Old Trafford:

March 1939 (Wolverhampton Wanderers versus Grimsby Town):
  76,962
March 2007 (Manchester United versus Blackburn Rovers): 76,098

In the antediluvian slime, from where the English emerged, the first pinstripe suit took shape. It was complete with a coloured silk handkerchief peeping out of the breast pocket to show character. That is the only explanation there is for the sense of history, continuity and tailored superiority that accompanies the pinstripe. It feels permanently English – had Alfred the Great risen from the dead and popped across to the Stock Exchange, that is what he would have worn.

It feels English because of the understated subtlety of it. White vertical stripes on a dark suit of blue, grey or black, sewn at the width of a pin, sometimes next to each other in pairs or triplets. Not too wide, bright or garish. It is a combination intended to imply breeding, balance and good sense.

More evidence of the antediluvian origins of this lies in the fact that nobody has much idea who first tailored the perfect pinstripe.

It seems to have descended, fully developed, cut and sewn in heaven, to the windows of Hawes & Curtis and the other tailors of Jermyn Street in London.

Closer examination shows that it actually emerged with bowler hats (from the hatter Lock & Co. in St James's) and with ironed creases in the trousers, an Edwardian innovation which is supposed to have been a mistake from drying Edward VII's wet pantaloons after an unexpected drenching.

Some theories suggest that the first pinstripes appeared via the equally English venue of Wimbledon as Edwardian tennis gear. It was certainly all about sport to start with – borrowed from Edward VII's relaxed sporting style – but the style came of age during the Great Depression. Edward VII's grandson Edward VIII made them popular when he was Prince of Wales. The ubiquitous pinstripe emerged as the apotheosis of conservative style in the City of London via the prince's Anglo-American fast set, glamourised by Hollywood thanks to a brief period on the backs of Chicago gangsters and hoodlums.

So thrilling were they when they caught on, that when Clark Gable wore a pinstripe suit on a visit to Buenos Aires in 1935, the lapels of his overcoat were torn off by overexcited female fans.

It took wartime austerity and the 1950s, with its sense of post-war inferiority, to make pinstripes what they are today. English City gents felt the need to assert some kind of superiority over their Wall Street cousins, and latched on to the pinstripe as the classic English look. They may not have been richer or more powerful, they may have presided over a national debt that could have sunk lesser islands below the waves, but they could at least have sartorial style. Call it the *Avengers* effect.

It was a style that emphasised effortless class, just as thin vertical stripes emphasise height and elongate the wearer. There are capacious trouser pockets, so that men can put their hands inside and effect a nonchalance.

The great age of the pinstripe was the City of London in the late 1980s, after the Big Bang deregulation. It became the uniform of effortless superiority again, of fat-cat salaries and share options, but with subtle codes attached. If the stripes were too close together, you looked naïve. If they were too wide apart, you looked boorish and brash. Just the right width and you could be put up for membership of any gentleman's club, without further examination. As long as you also wore sock suspenders.

Giving pinstripes to the world:

Cost at auction of Winston Churchill's pinstripe suit (2002):
£32,500
Most famous sporting pinstripes: The New York Yankees
Most famous political pinstripes: Indian prime minister Narendra Modi

The English obsession with raincoats is clearly a by-product of their fascination with the weather, but here there is bound to be some disappointment because – when it comes to rainwear – the English have always been followers and not leaders.

The word 'mackintosh' is a bit of a giveaway. The inventor of macks, the Glasgow surgeon James Syme, found that a product of coal tar called naphtha could melt India rubber and make it possible to use it for waterproofing. But Syme was too busy to exploit his discovery and the patent went to another Scot, a clerk turned inventor called Charles Macintosh (note the different spelling). Macintosh took out a patent for a process which glued together two layers of cloth with India rubber, making it waterproof – or at least making some progress in that direction.

It is then that the English began to get involved. Macintosh's company merged in 1830 with its Manchester rival, Thomas Hancock. Together they got a contract to supply the British army and the rest is history, in which Queen Victoria herself seems to have played a role.

Her Highland jaunts had changed people's attitude to the rain. If she could stride out in the Scottish drizzle wearing her sturdy Balmoral boots, just as William Wordsworth had done in the Lake District (Wordsworth had died in 1850), then so could everybody else. Charles Macintosh had patented his waterproofing process in 1823: his waterproofs snapped in the cold, were sticky in the heat and smelled horribly of naphtha, but at least they kept the rain out. The Basingstoke draper Thomas Burberry had managed a similar effect with a very tight weave in 1835.

Burberry still exists and so does the Mackintosh company, which was taken over by Dunlop in 1925 and stumbled on for another couple of generations. It was just as it was on the verge of closing its factory in Cumbernauld when, in the 1990s, it reinvented itself as a trendy fashion brand. It is now owned by the Japanese company Yagi Tsusho.

The truth is that the English have never managed to stamp their identity on to waterproof clothing in the way you would have expected. Anorak and parka are Inuit words, and carry an implication in English these days as clothes for obsessives and geeks. Cagoule is a French term for hood.

What dreadful hot weather we have! It keeps one in a continual state of inelegance.

Jane Austen, in the days before rainwear

I n the ancient world, roast beef was considered indigestible. There may be be some truth in this, but the English Renaissance food writers thought otherwise, on the grounds that beef wasn't the same everywhere. This is undoubtedly true too. Like a stopped clock, so the logic went, beef had to be palatable somewhere and it seemed sensible to suggest that this place might be England.

So much else about English cuisine has slipped into the country unawares. That explains the old ditty: 'hops, reformation, bays and beer / Came into England one bad year.' But beef has probably been here as long as cows, and that is quite a long time.

Yorkshire pudding is different. It was the cooks in the north of England who developed the idea of putting some wheat flour into the pan of dripping while the joints were bubbling away. The result was rather flatter than today's Yorkshire pudding – these days, they have to be at least four inches tall to qualify.

That explains the original name: 'dripping pudding'. It took the London cookery writer Hannah Glasse (1708–70) to reinvent this as 'Yorkshire pudding', in her famous but anonymous 1747 book *The Art of Cookery*. She spent her declining years in a debtors' prison, but managed to write another book which provided her with enough earnings to pay for her release. Ten years before, William Kenrick published what is perhaps the first effective recipe.

Make a good batter as for pancakes; put in a hot toss-pan over the fire with a bit of butter to fry the bottom a little then put the pan and butter under a shoulder of mutton, instead of a dripping pan, keeping frequently shaking it by the handle and it will be light and savoury, and fit to take up when your mutton is enough; then turn it in a dish and serve it hot.

Recipe for dripping pudding in William Kenrick,
  The Whole Duty of a Woman *(1737)*

f English food has had a poor reputation over the generations, then the absolute nadir – apart of course from the gruel meted out to Oliver Twist – is the experience of school dinners. English cabbage or carrots tended to be boiled to the point of indigestibility, and once the school-dinner ladies got their hands on vegetables, they really did have all flavour and most of the colour surgically removed.

Grown men have been known to cry at the memory of imminent tapioca pudding, or of sitting before it while it reached ambient temperatures, waiting for some solution that might possibly make it edible, while the school day passed by, with the remains of the peas and mash trodden into the school's lino.

'You will stay there until you eat it' is a phrase that carries within it the most appalling tolerance of the most dreadful creations known to culinary science. Of course you shouldn't eat it.

Those skimpy, translucent slices of meat, that sickly gravy, a few potatoes boiled to death. The mere thought of it can carry you back there, to the primary school at 1 p.m. on a Thursday, and the memory carries those of us from that generation of Englishness back through the decades to the smell of dying cabbage that used to impregnate the floors.

But don't let us forget that there is another side to school dinners before the government, in their infinite wisdom, decided to close the school kitchens and replace them with pre-cooked turkey twizlers trucked in from 200 miles away by a big contractor, which may as well have been Rentokil. At least we used to get a square meal at lunchtimes.

And there is another element to English school dinners that has an almost erotic feel to it – the school puddings. Ah yes, the huge great lumps of them, steaming on the plate under a thick, yellow layer of custard, great wads of suet and stodge, in chocolate, jam or currants, carrying a whiff of comfort so powerful that people still long for them years later. Especially on the endless evenings of an English winter.

Maybe English food is like its religion – and perhaps also its love-making. It is staggeringly, outrageously, middle-of-the-road. But perhaps in this sheer ordinariness, in the very drabness of its passion, there is something comforting too.

> Bean soup and bread, followed by treacle pudding
> Toad in the hole, potatoes and bread
> Mutton stew and suet pudding
> Fish and potato pie, followed by baked raisin pudding
>
> *School dinner menus, 1906*

You cannot hope to bribe or twist,
thank God! the British journalist.
But, seeing what the man will do
unbribed, there's no occasion to.

So wrote Humbert Wolfe, the British civil servant and poet of German–Italian descent, in 1930. He was referring in part to one of the strange paradoxes of English life – the bizarre division between the scribblers and propagandists and the exuberance of what we now know as the tabloid press, and the deep disapproval that they attract.

It is a paradox that goes back at least to 1662, and the first prosecution under the notorious Licensing Act, when John Twyn refused to give the name of the author of an anti-Royalist pamphlet he had published and was sentenced to be hanged, drawn and quartered. It was a fearsome punishment for publishing poor writing, and the tradition continued in earnest through 1961 and the Vassall spy case, when two journalists were jailed by a tribunal set up by Prime Minister Harold Macmillan for refusing to name their sources.

The more refined English have gargled with different words about this monster in their midst, threatening to reveal everything about them to the hoi polloi. Sometimes they call it 'the gutter press'. Sometimes it is the 'penny dreadfuls'. 'Tabloids' is just the latest word and the latest incarnation. The tabloids have invented a language all of their own, very exciting and simple, and created along with it a new kind of newspaper layout such as the one produced by Hugh Cudlipp at the *Daily Mirror* in the 1960s, and developed by Larry Lamb after his boss Rupert Murdoch snapped up the *Sun* in 1969.

It was energetic, raucous and it took up a lot of space. 'What's that doing?' asked Murdoch after his first edition rolled off the press, indicating the white space around the headlines.

'That's artistic white.'

'Well, I don't know how artistic it is but I do know it's cost a lot of trees.'

Tabloids also aspire to political power, as English popular journalism has always done, since Lord Northcliffe unveiled the *Daily Mail* in 1900. Lord Beaverbrook (a Canadian) managed to grasp quite a bit during both world wars, and Cecil King's Mirror Group Newspapers even advocated taking power by force after his headline 'Enough is enough!', aimed at Harold Wilson in 1968 (he was told off by Lord Mountbatten). Murdoch (an Australian and then an American) hardly needed to take power by force, since every politician with ambition was coming to him on bended knee, seeking advancement.

But it is the phenomenon of the tabloid headline that somehow sums it all up. 'Gotcha' wrote *Sun* editor Kelvin MacKenzie across the front page when the Argentine cruiser *General Belgrano* was sunk in 1982. The paper lost its nerve in later editions and changed the headline to 'Did 2,000 Argies die?' Hardly better, so perhaps it isn't surprising that 'Gotcha' makes repeat appearances in the paper's history.

The whole point of these headlines is that they should be in poor taste. One *Sun* headline in 1990 ran: '158 degrees: four-week twins roasted to death by electric blanket'.

The American writer Tom Wolfe included an English reporter, Peter Fallow, in his blockbuster novel *The Bonfire of the Vanities* (1987). Fallow was supposed to be working as a stringer in New York – a man of long lunchtimes and even longer hangovers. It was such a typical caricature that all the English members of the press in New York assumed that Fallow had been modelled on them. But the key point is that, to make it believable, Wolfe had to create an *English* pressman.

The tabloid style worked well in the USA for a time – see Jack Lemmon and Walther Matthau in *The Front Page* (1974) – but it doesn't amount to the breathtaking deviance of an English tabloid newspaper.

The reporters have occasionally hit back against their critics. The press corps at the Old Bailey at one stage sued for libel when a piece of prose described them collectively as 'beer-sodden hacks'. There certainly has been a traditional link between English reporting and alcoholism. The press veterans in the days when Fleet Street was Fleet Street would turn up to work, put their jacket on the back of their chair – to imply they were somewhere in the building, maybe studying at the cuttings library – and then head straight out to the pub. These days, perhaps not only Fleet Street, but also the Fleet Street bar El Vino, are not quite what they were.

On the other hand, the great divide between a po-faced establishment and a wildly excitable press corps, has something to do with the class war. As Larry Lamb said: 'I have worn throughout my life a substantial chip on my shoulder, on the grounds that I am not educated and I should have been.'

It was a revealing comment. The press corps managed to maintain a powerful, articulate and persuasive challenge to the establishment on behalf of the University of Life. It has certainly been rude, occasionally offensive, possibly even seditious. But it has at least kept them up to some kind of mark.

Believe nothing until it has been officially denied.

Claud Cockburn (though he denied it)

L ife in the City of London has never been exactly dull, but in the days of George II it was particularly colourful, and the most colourful figure of all was Jonas Hanway. Hanway always dressed as if he was on his way to a ball, with silk hose and silver-buckled shoes, carrying a large bag and wearing a broad-brimmed hat with lace trimmings, and a small sword with a golden hilt. For thirty years, he also carried a small Persian umbrella.

This used to enrage the coachmen, who believed it made him look French, and because they never liked new fashions – and because the traditional way of avoiding the rain in London, in those days, was to call a sedan chair. A generation after Hanway, another umbrella pioneer called John Macdonald used to be greeted with cries of 'Frenchman! Why don't you call a coach?'

It wasn't that Hanway invented umbrellas, which go back to ancient China around 1100 BC. But he was the first to dare to carry one in

London, and did so regardless of the abuse as he travelled the streets from his home in the Strand and then in Red Lion Square to his office in Bishopsgate. Paris fashions had already suggested that using parasols to keep the rain off might be wise, but the idea at the heart of the fashion – that weather is very uncertain – definitely suited the English.

Hanway was one of the great English social reformers, and traders. His contemporary Samuel Johnson said that 'he acquired some reputation by travelling abroad, but lost it all by travelling at home'.

Hanway was born at sea in 1712, though his parents lived in Portsmouth. He was disappointed in love in Portugal as a young man, and as a result remained unmarried for the rest of his life – which he spent as a City trader dealing first with St Petersburg, which involved his capture by the Swedes in the Baltic (they were at war with Russia at the time), and then travelling with a Tartar boy and some soldiers across the Caspian Sea with a consignment of cloth to trade with Persia. He wrote more than seventy books, including his pamphlets inveighing against the wasteful and unhealthy English habit of drinking tea.

Hanway is remembered almost entirely for championing the cause of the umbrella, when he ought to be remembered for being the first genuine social entrepreneur. He tackled schemes to prevent infanticide, and to take orphan children out of workhouses and send them to live in people's homes. He founded the Magdalen Asylum for retired prostitutes, and the Marine Society to train impoverished young chimney sweeps for a life at sea.

Which brings us back to umbrellas, which in Hanway's day and afterwards were cumbersome, damp oily things (his were made of Persian silk, of course) held together by whale bone with very long handles. It wasn't long before the logic of wielding an umbrella in

London became clear. But unless they were coloured black to start with, the smoky rain would very soon stain them that colour.

So it is partly dirt, and partly doubt about the weather, that made the black umbrella such a symbol of English life. And it became a paradoxical symbol as well, especially for those tough-minded English people who believed it was polite to keep your umbrella furled, whatever the weather.

The modern Jonas Hanway was Major Digby Tatham-Warter of the Parachute Regiment, who led his men against Nazi tanks during the fruitless battle for Arnhem, wearing a bowler hat and carrying an umbrella, with which he disabled an enemy tank. He claimed he carried it because he could never remember the password and an umbrella would reveal him unambiguously as English. It is said that, at the height of the battle – during which he was captured and escaped with the help of the Dutch resistance – he was asked whether the umbrella was much help. 'But, my goodness,' he replied. 'What if it rains?'

Virtue in humble life: containing reflections on relative duties, particularly those of masters and servants. Thoughts on the passions, prejudices, and tempers of mankind, drawn from real characters. Fables applicable to the subjects. Various anecdotes of the living and the dead in two hundred and nine conversations between a father and his daughter, amidst rural scenes, intended as an amusing and instructive library to persons of certain conditions and proper for all families seeking domestic peace and Christian piety, with a manual of devotion.

A book title by Jonas Hanway, 1777

There is something insufferably respectable about the Women's Institute, where the English middle classes – at least the female of the species, in tweed skirts – gather to discuss jam-making and other gentle, rural pursuits. This is of course, wholly unfair – did not the members of the Rylstone WI in Yorkshire strip off in a fundraising calendar in 1999? Did not the WI have the temerity to boo Tony Blair when he was prime minister? They did but, equally, the idea that the WI is wholeheartedly English to its very bones is not quite accurate. It actually began in Canada.

To be precise, it began in 1897 in Stoney Creek, Ontario, the brainchild of Adelaide Hoodless, who believed the idea would involve women when their menfolk were involved with the Farmers' Institute. There has always been a rural edge to the WI. Even when it arrived in the UK, the first branch wasn't in England at all. It was in Llanfairpwllgwyngyll in Anglesey in 1915, when the intention was to encourage more women to get involved in food production.

It was during the darkest days of the Second World War, when luxuries were extremely scarce, that WIs took on the role of making jam. They collected the fruit, often from hedgerows, and the government provided the tinning machines. It was a big responsibility and they rose to the challenge.

There are now over 200,000 members of WIs in England and Wales, and the organisation has become a ferocious campaigning force, at the same time as it is revitalising rural arts and crafts. It is one of the wooden walls of England. It even has 'Jerusalem' (see Chapter 37) as its anthem, inherited from the non-militant suffragist movement.

In recent years, there has been a trend for much younger women to launch their own urban WIs and it has given the movement a new lease of life. Sami Score founded the Iron Maidens WI in Liscard in Merseyside in 2012, including tattoos and various piercings. Most WIs are about self-sufficiency and mutual support, which in the English mind are rather peculiarly linked.

Ralph Vaughan Williams cantata, composed for the WI in 1952, included the following traditional English folk tunes:
'To the Ploughboy'
'May Song'
'To the Green Meadow'
'An Acre of Land'
'The Sprig of Thyme'
'Lark in the Morning'
'The Cuckoo'
'Wassail Song'

WINTER

The British Broadcasting Corporation has a global reputation for impartiality and truth and is well known the world over for being a byword for Britishness. This is not completely fair. The reputation for impartiality and truth was won the hard way during the Second World War, broadcasting to occupied Europe in thirty-six languages – still the biggest broadcasting operation in the history – but was carried out by the European Service under the control of the Foreign Office, having escaped BBC control altogether.

As for the Britishness, this is actually – and despite the full toolbox of regional accents – clearly Englishness. Yes, the BBC retains some of its Puritanism from its dour Scottish founding director general, John Reith. But its understated politeness, its obsessive political balance, is overwhelmingly English.

So it is strange that such an upright English institution, which feels sometimes as if it descended on a cloud from heaven shortly after the creation of the world, should have owed its existence to a stunt by a tabloid newspaper.

Tom Clarke, assistant to the *Daily Mail*'s founder, Lord Northcliffe, had been a signals officer in the First World War, which had been over for little more than eighteen months. It was he who suggested that the *Mail* should sponsor a radio broadcast. A few short musical broadcasts – even the train timetable read slowly over the crackling valves – had thrilled the handful of enthusiasts during the early months of 1920. The first licences had been issued through the Post

Office the previous year. Now Northcliffe leaped at the idea that they would organise something truly professional, and as soon as possible.

To that end, on 15 June 1920, the great soprano Dame Nellie Melba was transported to Chelmsford to sing into a microphone. She did, and listeners as far as Newfoundland were able to hear her (she never broadcast again once she discovered they could do so for free). They even recorded a record from the foot of the Eiffel Tower. It caught the public imagination. Wireless, as they called it in those days, had arrived. It was barely a quarter of a century since inventor Guglielmo Marconi had taken out a patent for a transmitter and receiver capable of making a bell ring in a secret black box.

The first regular broadcasts were transmitted from January 1922 by the Marconi Company's radio station 2MT, and shortly afterwards, from Marconi House in the Strand, the sound of 2LO – the forerunner of the BBC – first crackled through the ether to be picked up by the precise positioning of a cat's whisker. 2LO broadcast for one hour a day, repeated at teatime. Music was banned and, every seven minutes, there had to be a three-minute interval for official announcements.

There never were any official announcements, but the early listeners welcomed the breaks – or so it was said – so they could pop next door or upstairs or into the kitchen for a cup of tea.

By the time 2LO was on the air, the government was already struggling with the question of how to organise a better broadcasting system, while avoiding what they saw as the chaos of American wireless. The last thing the English wanted was anything too spontaneous or – heavens above – jazz. The biggest six companies interested in broadcasting formed a committee and, by 25 May 1922, the name British Broadcasting Company had been agreed, its shares available only to British manufacturing companies. It would be funded by a five-shilling levy on wireless sets.

The first BBC broadcast was a six o'clock news bulletin, also from Marconi House, on 14 November. In line with the government guidelines, no news was allowed that had not already been published in the newspapers. It was read twice, first quickly and then slowly with pauses, so people could take notes.

The rest is history. History, *ITMA*, *Blue Peter*, *Doctor Who* and Arthur Askey.

When I was under house arrest, it was the BBC that spoke to me – I listened.

Aung San Suu Kyi

'Not a drum was heard, not a funeral note . . .' The line from Charles Wolfe's poem is so familiar to generations of English schoolchildren, though perhaps less so today, that it fails to quite do its job. The rhythm is so powerful that the words no longer quite manage to conjure up the silence at dusk after the battle as the body of Sir John is laid to rest in his bloodied uniform.

Moore himself was from Cobham in Surrey, though he was actually Scottish. An oak tree grown from an acorn from the garden of his home still stands in a small park to commemorate him in the Spanish city of Corunna. Like Nelson before him, he had the reputation of being a humanitarian maverick. In command of the Kent coast when Napoleon was expected to invade, he built the Martello Towers, cut the Royal Military Canal and recruited 340,000 militia men to defend the South Downs. He also invented the light infantry.

In 1809, he was leading the British expeditionary force against Napoleon, defending Spain from invasion, outnumbered by the French in what was one of the longest retreats the British army has ever endured. When Moore reached the coast at Corunna, he found the rescue fleet had failed to arrive and the enemy was getting closer. He had already lost 5,000 men. This was an early version of Dunkirk, as Moore's remaining troops held back the French long enough to get away.

It was terrible January weather and Moore took a musketball in the shoulder, rather as Nelson had just over three years before, and spent the remainder of the battle dying in a fisherman's house where he had been taken in. Officially, his last words were: 'I hope the people of England will be satisfied! I hope my country will do me justice!'

Like many English heroes, Moore's official last words didn't quite square up with his real ones. Turning to his aide-de-camp, he said: 'Remember me to your sister, Stanhope.' This referred to the explorer Lady Hester Stanhope, providing a hint of evidence that they might have been in love.

Moore was buried wrapped in an army cloak next to the ramparts of the city. When the French commander Marshal Soult arrived, he ordered a memorial to be built to mark the spot.

Corunna was another of those typically English victories snatched from the jaws of defeat – or, more accurately, an escape snatched from the jaw of annihilation. It might not have been remembered at all, outside Corunna, where Moore remains a local hero, were it not for Charles Wolfe's poem, 'The Burial of Sir John Moore after Corunna'.

Nor was Wolfe actually English. He was from County Tyrone and a relative of the great Irish revolutionary Wolfe Tone. He published the poem after graduating and it appeared in a local paper in Newry in 1817. It was promptly forgotten until, some years after Wolfe's death, Byron found the poem and popularised it.

> Slowly and sadly we laid him down,
> From the field of his fame fresh and gory;
> We carved not a line, and we raised not a stone,
> But we left him alone with his glory.

Clothes have always been political in England. The New Look dresses of the late 1940s shocked public taste with their sumptuous sense of luxury. The miniskirt was a sign of liberation for women in the 1960s, just as bicycling skirts were a symbol of much the same thing for their grandmothers. The great art critic John Ruskin imagined a return to the medieval sumptuary laws which laid down which class was allowed to wear what. But the English, being an awkward race, would have none of it.

We may be conventional in our dress, unless we are in the tropics as Noël Coward pointed out ('Although the English are effete / They're quite impervious to heat'), but we don't like being told what to wear. There is something of the servant–master relationship about it, as if we were being asked to wear livery.

The advent of cloth caps – now such a symbol, paradoxically, of both working-class and upper-middle-class life – began with one of the last of these dress codes, In 1571, during the reign of Elizabeth I, Parliament legislated to support the wool industry by boosting the consumption of wool. All men over the age of six had to wear some kind of what was then called a woollen 'bonnet' on Sundays and holidays. The only people who were exempted, apart from women and babies of course, were 'persons of degree'. If ordinary people didn't wear a cap they were fined three farthings, and those were the days when three quarters of a pence was the value of a pint of beer or a chicken

The law stayed on the statute book for nearly three decades and, by the time it was repealed, cloth caps had become a symbol of respectability – of people prepared to keep the law, of upright citizenship and successful bourgeois trade. The Tudor bonnet was so popular that it remains part of some forms of academic dress today, so if you have been awarded a PhD at some universities, you have to wear a Tudor version of the cloth cap made out of black velvet.

By the early twentieth century, most men still wore hats and the cloth cap was widely adopted by a range of classes, and for golfers in particular, on both sides of the Atlantic – and especially for boys, who (if they were anything like me) chafed and rebelled at the mere prospect. The old Tudor bonnet had become a symbol to say 'I am a person of degree'. You will still see the Prince of Wales wearing one, or David Beckham, just as you will see the same thing on the head of Andy Capp or Del-Boy Trotter. It is peculiarly paradoxical, a symbol of class identity which is actually worn by almost every class.

The cap is traditional wear for American newsboys too, though often with a button on the top, and for older men in South Korea or Irishmen in Boston. It is worn back to front in some forms of hip-hop culture and by Hollywood figures like Robert Redford, and other people who hail from California. The Canadian and American teams at recent Olympic events have been dressed in specially designed red or white flat caps.

But above all else, it is a symbol of working-class English life in the mid-twentieth century. There is a famous photograph of the workforce returning from lunch at the shipbuilding yard of John Brown & Co. in Clydebank, filing up the gangplanks on to the hulk of the liner *Queen Mary* as the ship was being built in 1935, having started work again a few months before with a huge government loan to support Clydeside through the Great Depression. Not one head lacks the not-so-distinctive cloth cap.

Pubs in Yorkshire have been ordered to ban people from wearing flat caps or other hats so troublemakers can be more easily recognised.

Daily Telegraph, *June 2008*

When James Watt, the Scottish pioneer, first cracked the business of making an efficient steam engine, it gave coal the status in the English economy and in English life that wool had won for itself in the Middle Ages. It underpinned not just the Industrial Revolution, but all the production and manufacturing that followed. For centuries, the coal man, with his black face and black sacks, was a familiar sight in any street, pouring the black gold down a hole in the pavement. For decades, the dirty business of coaling ships was as much a part of the seagoing life as sails in the breeze. And, of course, the miners struggled half-naked, hundreds of feet below ground, with lamps in their hats, to support the English on the ground above.

During the twentieth century, the appearance of miners – complete with lamps on their hats – would bring a standing ovation at any radical political rally. The last stand of the miners, in the disastrous strike of 1984–5, has entered folk legend.

It was for this reason, perhaps, that Sir Humphrey Davy, one of the inventors of the miners' safety lamp – an honour he shares partly with George Stephenson – became practically a new saint in the English calendar in the nineteenth century.

Coal was mentioned by Aristotle, so it is hardly uniquely English. There are also many different kinds of coal, all of which behave in different ways when burned. Even so, mining for coal seems to have begun in England back in the Stone Age. Archaeologists have found coal cinders in Roman camps, and we know that Newcastle was given a royal charter by Henry III to mine the stuff in 1239.

By 1306, London's air had become so disgusting – a great London tradition which continues to this day – that Edward I went so far as to ban sea coal. This lasted only long enough for Londoners to cut down all the trees within the vicinity of the city, and then the coal was back. It is one of the peculiar themes of English life through the ages: an overwhelming tolerance of dirt. And grime, smoke and soot – and 'Chim Chim Cher-ee' from *Mary Poppins*, a film which at least gives chimney sweeps their proper place in the scheme of things.

'Get up!' the caller calls, 'Get up!'
And in the dead of night,
To win the bairns their bite and sup,
I rise a weary wight.

My flannel dudden donn'd, thrice o'er
My birds are kiss'd, and then
I with a whistle shut the door
I may not ope again.

Joseph Skipsey (1832–1903),
the 'Pitman Poet'

Until the end of the Middle Ages, the patron saint of England used to be – not St George – but St Edward the Confessor, the only English king to be canonised. This was wholly undeserved: he was regarded by the church as particularly holy because of his apparent decision not to procreate, though he actually locked his wife up as a punishment for her failure to do so.

So cast your mind back, if you will, to St Edward's Day, 13 October 1257, when Henry III decided he would hold a Fish Day in celebration. Fish was considered holy too, as it wasn't meat, and his household gathered together and ate 250 bream, 300 pike and 15,000 eels, collected from all over the country. These were the days when a staggering number of different fish were eaten, even porpoise (not strictly fish, but treated as one), distributed right into the English Midlands.

Now here is the point of this slight digression: English fish – like everything else English – had a kind of class system about them. There were the fish that kings and nobles ate, like porpoise or carp, dressed in luxurious cream sauces. There were the fish the gentry ate: herring and cod and the salted fish known as stockfish, which eventually earned England so much of the gold and silver fetched from the New World. As for the poor, they tended to make do with eels or cockles, whelks and oysters.

These were gathered on the coast, usually by women, pickled and distributed inland. Seafood of this kind remained a staple food of the poor in England into the last century. By Victorian times, the whelks were brought to London and the cities, boiled alive and then sold by itinerant salesman or on stalls, along with hot eels – sold spicy 'as if there was gin in it'.

One whelk-stallholder told the writer Henry Mayhew that the whelks accepted being boiled alive. 'They never kicks as they boils,' he said, 'like lobsters or crabs. They takes it quiet.' They weren't eaten to fill you up, but as a little luxury, from jars carried round pubs, eaten with a little pepper and vinegar; the Victorian equivalent of a bag of crisps.

> Of all merry blades that ply merry trades,
> Or win the affections of pretty young maids;
> There is no one so trim or supple of limb
> As light-hearted, ruddy-faced mussel man, Jim.
> My musical sounds enliven my rounds,
> I'm known the world over, from Stepney to Bow;
> While singing aloud to a wondering crowd,
> Fresh Cockles and Mussels alive, alive O!
>
> J. B. Geoghagen, 'Jim the Mussel Man' (1876)

The final decades of the nineteenth century, when the biggest demographic earthquakes in English society were under way, coincided with the rising popularity of the pantomime about Dick Whittington and his cat. Whittington is a kind of patron saint for all those millions who made the journey from the rural life and found that the city streets were not in fact paved with gold – but who managed to scrape together a living anyway.

Whittington arrived penniless in London, his only asset – or so the story goes – a cat with a particular skill at catching mice. One thing leads to another and the cat makes Dick's fortune with the support of a wealthy merchant, whose daughter he marries. It is a very English story, and particularly it reeks of London – where the sound of the bells in 'Oranges and Lemons' all seems to be about debts and the interest paid on them. These are the bells that are supposed to have drawn Whittington and his cat back to London: 'Turn again, Whittington,' said the Great Bell of Bow, and it made him more than a living. He was a hugely successful merchant, operating out of the Mercers' Company, selling cloth to Europe, and – like so many in London – a financier.

Actually, as so often, the story about Dick Whittington founding his fortune by lending out his cat, who dealt so effectively with the mice, was not originally English at all: it is based on a Persian story. The real Whittington was born sometime in the 1350s in the Forest of Dean and really was mayor of London four times, imposed on the city by Richard II to settle his dispute with the merchants. He really did marry Alice Fitzwarren, as the stories say, in 1402. He died two decades later, extremely wealthy and founding a charity that still shells out money to this day.

There is a story that he lent Henry V most of the money he needed to invade France, then – after the great victory at Agincourt – he invited the king to dinner and ceremonially burned the debt papers in the fire next to the table.

But what was the connection between Whittington and cats? A mummified cat was found where he was buried in the church of St Michael Paternoster Royal, but that seems to have been put there some centuries later. There is also a cat in the portrait of him in the hall of the Mercers' Company. Maybe he just liked them. There is one other story: there was a merchant called Dick Whittington a century or so later, who was involved in one contract to import four lions from Africa into England for Henry VII. He can't have been the same man, who died anyway in 1423, but he may have been some kind of relative. The historian David Quinn suggested that here was the origin of the legendary linking of Whittington and cats. We will never know.

> Turn again, Whittington,
> Once Lord Mayor of London!
> Turn again, Whittington,
> Twice Lord Mayor of London!
> Turn again, Whittington,
> Thrice Lord Mayor of London!
>
> *What Bow Bells said to Dick Whittington*

Ten days after the Armistice in 1918, the British Grand Fleet steamed out of its safe anchorage at Scapa Flow to take the surrender of the German battle fleet. It was a misty day in the North Sea as the battleships waited for the encounter and a tense moment. The ships were cleared for action and it was widely believed that, when the moment came, the German battleships would not in fact surrender.

As they came into view, steaming in a long grey line, they were sighted on the new battleship HMS *Royal Oak*, manned by men from Plymouth and flying the flags made by the ladies of Devonshire. It was at that moment, and often again over the next few hours, that those on the bridge heard the unmistakable beating of a drum.

The *Royal Oak* was flagship of the First Battle Squadron. When it was clear that the German fleet was going to surrender safely, the admiral mentioned the drum. The other senior officers had heard it too and couldn't understand it. Two searches of the ship were carried out for the mysterious drummer, who should have been at action stations. Nobody was found. The conclusion was that this had been Drake's Drum.

There are actually three Drake's Drums. The first was the drum which went everywhere with Sir Francis Drake on his circumnavigation of the world, and was with him when he died off the coast of Panama in 1596. It is now kept safely somewhere in central England. The second is the exact replica made with original materials, and painted also with Drake's family coat of arms, which is kept in a glass case in his home at Buckland Abbey in Buckland Monachorum in Devon. The third is a little more peculiar – it is the strange sound of a drum that is supposed to beat when England is in danger, last heard – or so it is said – during the retreat to Dunkirk in 1940, and so memorably on board the *Royal Oak*.

Drake's Drum is the stuff of Edwardian romance. It is said that Drake himself urged that the drum be taken home, and if England was ever in danger, we were to beat it and summon him up from the afterlife to its defence. Sir Henry Newbolt, the doyen of Edwardian romanticism, even wrote a poem about it – and it was then set to music by Charles Stanford. In fact, the reported instances of it sounding do not seem to be always when England is in danger but when the danger's over – when Nelson was given the freedom of the city of Plymouth and when Napoleon arrived there as a prisoner.

Drake himself is an ambiguous character to choose as a national hero. He had derring-do in abundance, but he might be described today more like a terrorist – or a slave trader, which he undoubtedly was.

Take my drum to England, hang et by the shore,
Strike et when your powder's runnin' low.
If the Dons sight Devon, I'll quit the port o'
    Heaven,
An' drum them up the Channel as we drummed
    them long ago.

Henry Newbolt, 'Drake's Drum' (1897)

One wintry morning in 1864, the sentry on duty at the Bloody Tower, one of the many outposts of the Tower of London, was found to be asleep. This is a serious charge for a soldier and he was duly court-martialled. It turned out that he had an elaborate defence.

He claimed that, in the early hours of that morning, he had been confronted outside by a terrifying apparition in white, seen clearly through the mist as a bonnet without a head inside, moving slowly towards him. He challenged the ghost three times and, when it still continued to approach, he lunged at it with his bayonet. There had been a strange flash and fire spread up his rifle, after which he passed out.

It looked like an embroidered excuse and the verdict looked a clear-cut one of guilty. But a number of soldiers, and one officer, came forward and gave evidence that they had seen something very similar – a white spirit in a headless bonnet – seen from the window at the Bloody Tower. A historian gave evidence that the guardroom had been immediately below the room where Anne Boleyn had spent her final night on earth, before being beheaded by a special swordsman brought from France for the task in 1536. The sleeping soldier was cleared of all charges.

England is not a very superstitious country. In fact, the English have traditionally looked down their noses at most superstitions, from walking under ladders to the kind of religious mumbo-jumbo they held in such horror in the Roman Catholic Church. Yet for some reason, belief in ghosts is very widespread in England – and so are the ghosts. The nation appears to be packed with grey ladies, blue ladies, sad-looking monks and weeping widows. There are playful ghosts and whole casts of actor ghosts, especially in the Theatre Royal Drury Lane, where the ghost tends to appear to herald a runaway hit.

There is a particular English habit of seeing the ghosts of people at the point of their death, which the Victorians and Edwardians particularly specialised in – previous generations would not have known about the moment of death, after all. Vice Admiral Sir George Tryon appeared at a dinner party in his own house in Eaton Square the moment he sank beneath the waves off the coast of Lebanon, along with his flagship HMS *Victoria* in 1893.

The Tower of London is, in fact, particularly ghostly. There may even be more ghosts there than the living, going right back to 1241 when a priest first saw the ghost of Thomas Becket. Henry VIII himself has been bayoneted by a guard as well, and relatively recently. The white headless bonnet was last seen in 1933.

Is it that the English are particularly credulous? I don't believe so. Apart from All Hallows' Eve, they have no day of the dead as other cultures do. No, the explanation, if there is one, is that England was one of the most westerly countries in the known world, and the utmost west used to be known as the resting place of the dead. It just so happened that the English made their homes there.

When the great ghost-story writer M. R. James, author of 'Oh, Whistle and I'll Come to You, My Lad' and other eerie tales, carried out a survey of how many of the English population had actually seen a ghost, it turned out that ten per cent claimed they had.

The dark and stormy nights that are such a feature of English life demand some kind of supernatural story, and the English have supplied them – originally via middle-class Victorian magazines like *Blackwood's* and others, and then thanks to Lord Halifax, who collected them from friends. Consequently, the ghost industry just keeps on growing. Sadly, the most haunted house in England, said to have been Borley Rectory in Essex, no longer stands. It was demolished in 1944.

Most haunted three places in England:

Tatton Old Hall, Cheshire
Ye Olde King's Head, Chester
Drakelow Tunnels, Kidderminster

According to Yvette Fielding, Radio Times, *2014*

The ancient wall that snakes across northern England from Wallsend to the Solway Firth has become an overwhelmingly English phenomenon, our very own answer to the Great Wall of China. But it is, almost by definition, a foreign import. The seventy-mile structure was ordered by the emperor Hadrian as a northern limit to the Roman Empire, and he seems to have inspected its progress on a visit in 122. Hadrian himself was hardly English either. In fact, he came from somewhere near Seville and was a huge admirer of Greek culture.

Those Roman troops posted to one of the frontier forts, who stared out from the battlements looking north, freezing with the snow on their bare legs, shivering as they peered into the blackness, were mostly not from here either. Maybe they became so from habit, like so many others in the centuries that followed.

But the strange thing about Hadrian's Wall, which seems to have been painted white when it was first built – in order to awe the watching tribes of the far north with its decorative simplicity – is that it seems to have been rather a comfortable place. Recent archaeology reveals that it was very unlike a frontier for most of its history. There were farms on either side of the wall, and a burgeoning Romano-British economy of hangers-on around it. Some of the farms had fields on the other side. It was not actually the limit to civilisation that the English might like to believe. It was rather a cosmopolitan party. At least, it was the kind of party you get when people come from all corners of the known world to organise an armed customs post in the middle of, well, somewhere.

Some evidence of the party emerges from messages inviting people to birthday parties discovered at Vindolanda fort, and written just after the fort was built as a preliminary for building the wall. They reveal a little of what it must have been like:

> Claudia Severa to her Lepidina greetings. On 11 September, sister, for the day of the celebration of my birthday, I give you a warm invitation to make sure that you come to us, to make the day more enjoyable for me by your arrival, if you are present (?). Give my greetings to your Cerialis. My Aelius and my little son send him (?) their greetings. I shall expect you, sister. Farewell, sister, my dearest soul, as I hope to prosper, and hail. To Sulpicia Lepidina, wife of Cerialis, from Severa.

A recent study found that the number of times the word 'Marmite' has been used in the press, when it is used as a metaphor for things which everyone either loves or hates, has shot up in an extraordinary way over the past decade. This is a testament to the marketing genius of Marmite, which used the commonplace idea that everyone either loves or hates Marmite as part of its marketing in 1996.

The stolid English, who actually agree on most things, need to boast about something they disagree about which is safe and actually pretty non-controversial. There will be no United Nations Security Council meetings of people who disagree about Marmite, after all. Marmite is the answer.

It is part of a package which includes the yellow lids, the broad bulbous pots, the brown stain on the toast, which now add up to something that feels overwhelmingly English. Actually, as so often, what seems obviously English is really nothing of the kind.

The discovery that brewer's yeast could be bottled and eaten was made originally by a German scientist called Justus von Liebig. The name Marmite was taken from the French word for large cooking pot, of the kind that still graces their labels. It is true that the product itself began in England, in Burton upon Trent in 1902 – the same year as the first teddy bear and the first borstal – but is now owned by the Anglo-Dutch food conglomerate Unilever, which has held the purse strings since 2000. Marmite had been bought decades before by the even more obviously English brand Bovril, whose marketing genius had come up with the slogan 'It prevents that sinking feeling' in 1920 (what sinking feeling, you ask?)

But the link with brewing gives Marmite an English edge. The yeast was originally provided by the brewers Bass, and it was so successful that a second factory was opened in 1907 at Vauxhall in south London.

The growth of Marmite was given a huge boost by two major twentieth-century events. The first was the First World War, which happened to coincide with the discovery that Marmite was rather a good way of treating vitamin B deficiency. It was therefore issued to troops on the Western Front and instantly became a symbol of nostalgia for those days of trench camaraderie. It was also issued to German prisoners of war during the Second World War (whether they liked it or hated it).

The second event was the discovery by the English scientist Lucy Wills, who discovered that Marmite could be used to treat anaemia among mill workers in Bombay, and it was therefore used to help tackle the famine a few years later in Sri Lanka.

It was these vitamins and additives, folic acid and vitamin B, that has also caused controversy more recently, especially when the Danish government refused to license it and Marmite was withdrawn from sale in Denmark. The outraged English press said that it had been banned, which wasn't quite accurate, but it was clearly a blow to national pride.

The opposite appeared to be happening in New Zealand around the time of the Christchurch earthquake in 2012 when the local factory was forced to shut down causing a national Marmite shortage. One report suggested that pots were changing hands at anything up to 800 New Zealand dollars.

Yet there is something comfortably English about Marmite – in the same category as scrambled eggs and bacon and Bakewell tarts – comfortable, reassuring, wintry and warm.

It was pretty good. It's just one of those things – you get out of the country and it's all you can think about.

Paul Ridout, a backpacker kidnapped in India by Kashmiri separatists,
describing his first Marmite on toast after his release,
from the Guardian, *1994*

The English adore cross-dressing. It is a repeated theme in Shakespeare plays, where it is never entirely clear what gender the person before you is going to turn into. It is there in traditional comedies like *Charley's Aunt* (1892) and it is there, Christmas after Christmas, in the bizarre phenomenon of the pantomime dame.

Of course, there is nothing very English about pantomimes, which derive from masked dramas in classical times, but the English have made them their own. The role of the pantomime dame – either high camp (John Inman) or butch (Les Dawson) – seems to have been pioneered by the great clown Joseph Grimaldi, who also popularised clowning so successfully that his name 'Joey' became – for a few generations – the word for clown. He clowned so spectacularly that it seems to have led to his physical collapse, alcoholism and early death.

Grimaldi was born in London, though his Italian grandfather came to London via France from Italy, having been imprisoned in the Bastille for offending Parisian tastes.

It was Grimaldi who invented the famous English catchphrase 'Here we are again!' It was he who first turned to the audience with a mischievous eye and said: 'Shall I?' Grimaldi, incidentally, was also responsible for the most disastrous pantomime in English theatrical history. He had taken the part of Grimaldicat in the 1818 Easter pantomime *Puss in Boots*. It closed after just one night. Grimaldi was booed off the stage after he pretended to eat a mouse on stage, and caused two women in the audience to fight.

But then it was appropriate that these traditions should have been brought here by Italians, because of the unbroken dramatic tradition stretching back to Roman mimes, followed by the characters of Renaissance theatre – Harlequin and Pantaloon, Pierrot and Columbine. In fact, when Francis Bacon talked about the tradition, he called it *pantomimi*.

Pantomimes in England date back to Boxing Day 1717, at Lincoln's Inn Fields Theatre, where the curtain raised on the first English panto, *Harlequin Executed*. It was the brainchild of the impresario John Rich, whose father has been forced out of Drury Lane and exhausted by rebuilding a new theatre around the corner, and decided to take them on with a 'new Italian mimic scene (never performed before) between a Scaramouch, a Harlequin, a Country Farmer, his Wife and others'. Rich played the Harlequin himself, and we can imagine that the farmer's wife provided the basis for what eventually became the dame.

There is a conspiracy theory about this, which suggests that – under the influence of Rich – the Harlequin was the main pantomime character. Under the influence of Grimaldi, a century later, it was the Clown, but after Grimaldi's death in 1837 there was rather a shortage of clowns. There was therefore a need to find some other kind of comic turn. Thus the pantomime dame was born.

The conspiracy theory is only partly true because Grimaldi pioneered the dame himself, and – after his death – it took at least another generation for pantomime dames to emerge in their full glory. The first dame of modern times was James Rogers, who took the part of Widow Twankey in *Aladdin* at the Strand Theatre in 1861.

Widow Twankey is usually portrayed as the manager of a Chinese laundry, which allows endless opportunities to laugh at people's underclothes (a major English pastime). This was a role that Grimaldi himself had invented back in 1813, but it took half a century for it to emerge in all its ferocity.

Dan Leno, the famous Victorian comic, took the role of Widow Twankey in the Theatre Royal Drury Lane in 1890, playing opposite Marie Lloyd as principal boy, and pantomime dames have never been the same since. The camp element was introduced by the cabaret artist Douglas Byng, who pioneered the part playing Eliza in *Dick Whittington* at the New Theatre in Oxford in 1924, and carried on for about half a century. He used the slogan 'Bawdy but British' and sang songs like 'Sex Appeal Sarah', 'Milly the Messy Old Mermaid' and 'The Lass who Leaned against the Tower of Pisa'.

> So here you are, old Douglas, a derelict at last.
> Before your eyes what visions rise of your vermilion past.
> Mad revelry beneath the stars, hot clasping by the lake.
> You need not sigh, you can't deny, you've had your bit of cake.
>
> *Douglas Byng's epitaph, which he wrote himself, before he died in Brighton at the age of ninety-three*

THE OLD CASTLE

The oldest legal code in existence, written by King Hammurabi in Babylon around 1750 BC, included a condemnation about overpriced, watered-down beer. In fact, the one universal opinion in the history of brewing is that the beer isn't as good as it was.

This implies that pubs are especially English in more ways than one. They are havens of contemplative companionship, but the basic conservatism of beer-drinking – beer drinkers are always dreaming of a better yesterday – puts pubs on the front line of two very English disputes. These are between the doyens of Merrie England and the two forces dedicated to ruining their good time – the puritans and the profiteers.

Nor should we assume that the puritan approach just comes from the forces of control and narrow-mindedness that English culture seems to revel in. Landlords are some of the biggest reactionaries ever invented. 'Shall I tell you why not?' a landlord told me recently when I asked for green tea. 'Because we're a pub.'

Fair enough, perhaps. The great English busybodies objected to the idea that, throughout the Middle Ages, anyone could open a pub under English law, so – if it was disorderly – Henry VII gave magistrates the power to close them down. The stage was set for the peculiar licensing system we have today which dates back ironically to the days of Bloody Mary, so that 'none after the first day of May next coming, shall be admitted or suffered to keep any common Ale-house or Tippling-house, but such as shall thereunto be admitted and allowed in open Sessions of the peace, or else by two Justices of the Peace'. You can hear, in those words of Renaissance legalese, the authentic voice of English bureaucracy.

There is an argument that the forces of control were redoubled by the arrival of James I from Scotland in 1603. It was certainly a concern under the Stuarts, but it was the Long Parliament of the 1640s – firmly under the control of the People – that first saw taxes on beer, 'for their own good' according to one of the Victorian treatises on the subject.

Merrie England hit back, and there were riots over attempts to control gin-houses in the 1730s and the first limits to opening hours for pubs in the 1860s (oddly enough, arrests for being drunk and disorderly doubled after the first restrictions). But the puritans took the opportunity of the First World War to take decisive action on pubs, because they were worried about drinking affecting the working habits of munitions workers. As a result, the Defence of the Realm Act in 1914 allowed the government to set pub opening hours. The following year, they were set at 12 noon to 2.40 p.m. for lunch, and 6.30 p.m. to 9.30 p.m. for supper.

But even that failed to undermine the pubs. In fact, the ritual of 'last orders' and 'Time, gentlemen, please!' went into the language – at least until it was swept away in 2005.

In the end, it appears to be the other battle which is finally corroding the pubs. The iron grip which the breweries held over the pub trade was loosened in the 1980s, only to be replaced by the monopolistic grip of the pub companies, which overvalued the properties in the boom years, got into unrepayable debt, and have been trying to extract it from their customers and their poor licensees ever since. Hence the darkened, shuttered pubs, especially in the cities. By 1823, there had been getting on for 49,000 pubs in England and Wales, or one for every 260 people. Now it is more like one for every 1,000 people.

But then the puritans were not completely wrong either. There is some disturbing link between the English and alcohol, which has been recognised across Europe at least since the twelfth century – where a surviving guidebook describes each nationality: the English, they say, are always drunk – and have 'tails'.

What the tails meant is anyone's guess, but the drunkenness remains. Perhaps it doesn't matter compared to the tankard and the open fire, and the traditional companionship of pub life, and the old pub signs creaking in the wind outside – witness to 1,000 years of history (one historian, Samuel Wildman, argued that the sign of the 'Black Horse' went back to King Arthur's day).

There remains something about an authentic English pub – if you can find them after wading through the fake beams and horse brasses, the books and pictures bought in bulk from house clearances. They are still deeply conservative places, as witnessed by the story told in 1972 by the writer Ben Davis about watching a woman eating lunch without having bought a drink. 'Can I have a glass of water then?' she said. 'What do you want?' said the landlord. 'A fucking wash or something?'

Oldest pubs:

Old Ferryboat Inn, Holywell, Cambridgeshire (560)

Ye Olde Fighting Cocks, St Albans (eighth century)

Bingley Arms, Bardsey (905)

Nag's Head, Burntwood (1086)

Ye Olde Salutation Inn, Nottingham (1240)

Adam and Eve, Norwich (1249)

Ye Olde Man and Scythe, Bolton (1251)

Eagle and Child, Stow-in-the-Wold (thirteenth century)

George Inn, Norton St Philip (fourteenth century)

New Inn, Gloucester (about 1450)

Ye Olde Trip to Jerusalem, Nottingham (disputed)

> Her face all bowsy
> Comely crinkled
> Like a roast pig's ear
> Bristled with hair.

Description of alewife Elinour Rumming of Leatherhead,
by poet John Skelton, 1508

There is something about roly-poly pudding that conjures up the winter in England, the strange metallic taste of school dinners and the sweet warmth of custard. Ah yes, the comfort of black and white television and Formica tables – it all comes wafting back.

There is a reason why roly-poly pudding is a winter dish. It is because it uses up the surplus fruits and jams from the summer. It also fits neatly into the need for warmth and stodge as the evenings have drawn in and the season of mist and mellow fruitfulness has given way to cold.

It belongs with the other great English puddings, spotted dick and sticky toffee pudding, which survive in rather old-fashioned cafes and restaurants, but which disappeared from many English dinner tables sometime in the 1970s. This kind of monstrosity always rather scared other nations – what was all this stodge about? – and it horrified the French because of its sheer weight. It horrified some Americans because of its defiance of everything that is politically correct in the way of healthy food.

Roly-poly puddings stretch back into the dawn of English puddings, which began as savoury concoctions in the medieval period, and evolved via Bakewell tarts to become the great sweet plate-fillers of the nineteenth century. Jam roly-poly pudding, as Mrs Beeton called it, probably emerged two centuries ago, with a combination of jam and large quantities of suet.

Suet is a key ingredient. So Atora suet went on sale at the end of the nineteenth century and still sells 2,400 tonnes a year. What isn't so easy to manage these days is the steaming. Most people pop them in the oven for baking. The puddings also no longer find themselves wrapped in old shirt-sleeves, which explains the less palatable name of Dead Man's Arm.

The most famous roly-poly pudding comes in Beatrix Potter's book *The Tale of Samuel Whiskers* (1908), which was first published with the title *The Roly-Poly Pudding*, so central was it to the plot. Samuel Whiskers was the name of the Potter pet rat, much lamented, which had died some years before. Whiskers and his compatriots take Tom Kitten hostage and roll him up in pastry. He is rescued in the nick of time by the carpenter. It would have been a terrible, and yet tremendously English fate.

Baked roly-poly recipe:

Preheat the oven to 200°C / gas mark 6 and line a baking tray with baking paper. In a large bowl, mix together 250 g plain flour, 2 teaspoons baking powder, 1 pinch salt and 2 tablespoons caster sugar. Stir in 125 g shredded suet and enough water to create a soft, but not sticky dough. Use a floured surface to roll dough into a 30 x 20 cm oblong shape. Brush with 4 tablespoons of jam, leaving a 1–2 cm border all around. Brush the border with egg wash made from an egg beaten with a tablespoon of milk. Roll the dough into a loose roll, starting at the short side. Pinch the ends to seal. Transfer to prepared baking tray seam side down. Brush with egg wash and sprinkle with sugar. Bake in the oven for 35–40 minutes or until golden and cooked through. Serve hot with custard.

It is September 1660, the restored king is on the throne, and the great diarist Samuel Pepys is about to test out a whole new element of Englishness: 'did send for a Cupp of Tee (a China drink) which I had never drunk before'.

Now there is something strange about this. Pepys is pretty clear that he thinks of tea as a foreign concoction, yet it is hard to imagine anything so quintessentially English as a cup of it. If the English were the magpies of the world, collecting bits and pieces around the planet to enhance their culture – and they clearly were – then there is really nothing quite as contradictory as tea-drinking.

On the face of it, it is hard to imagine anything quite so un-English. How could a drink described by the Chinese emperor Chin-Nung in 2,737 BC as the 'cup that cheers' find its way into the English soul? Yet there was Pepys, testing out the beverage brought to English high society that very year, by Charles II's Portuguese bride Catherine of Braganza, whose vast dowry had to be paid partly in spices and other eastern delicacies, including 'tea'.

The first advertisement for tea had appeared in London two years before (23 September, since you ask). Already the Dutch East India Company was paying doctors to recommend it as a health drink – one Dutch doctor recommended 200 cups a day.

But how did it become so overwhelmingly English? The answer is partly: *by accident*. The English East India Company was thrown out of the warehouses on Java in 1684, and their representatives were forced to import tea directly from China, which turned out to be much quicker and therefore much less expensive. At the same time, they were under political pressure back home to stop undermining the English textiles market, and they began to compensate their Indian traders by cultivating tea in Assam.

In London society, something alchemical was happening. Women were banned from the man's world of coffee houses, so they made tea-drinking their very own, sipping the stuff in tiny porcelain teacups the size of thimbles, packed with sugar from the American plantations. They even adopted the Parisian habit of adding a drop of milk.

The first teahouse in England opened in 1717, the Golden Lyon at 217 Strand. Not many decades later, Samuel Johnson described himself as a 'hardened and shameless Tea-drinker, who has for twenty years diluted his meals with only the infusion of this fascinating plant, whose kettle scarcely has time to cool, who with Tea amuses the evening, with Tea solaces the midnight, and with Tea welcomes the morning'. In 1678, Henry Savile complained about people 'who call for teas instead of pipes and bottles after dinner – a base unworthy Indian practice'. Then a century later, the philosopher Jeremy Bentham proposed tea as a way to reform criminals.

The English may have adopted a foreign drink, but they also left their mark on tea. The Victorians soon dispensed with green tea and embraced the black stuff, grown in Wuyi in north-west Fujian, and carried by Chinese workers in lead-lined boxes over the mountains, and then on to Canton or Shanghai.

From there it would be bought or rejected by a handful of foreigners, mainly British and Americans, who were allowed to live in a tiny area outside Canton as buyers and agents. Then there were three or four months running home on clippers (Captain Robertson of the Victorian tea clipper *Cairngorm* never slept during the home run, just napping on a deckchair on the poop deck). The tea was poured out on the floor in the Port of London, tested for adulteration, and brewed by a professional tea-taster, before being bought, packaged and shipped out to the hearths of England.

After that, it was brought out for the wealthy at tea dances and other At Home functions, and for the working classes for 'high tea' after the shift had ended – cold potatoes and veg and scalding hot tea. Or it was sold in cups at Lyons' Corner Houses (first one: 213 Piccadilly in 1894) for actresses and clergymen alike.

In fact, it was a teahouse liaison between actresses and the clergyman the Rev. Mr Harold Davidson that led to dismissal from his position as Rector of Stiffkey in Norfolk in 1932, and his famous demise in Skegness as a lion tamer, at the hands of a lion. Tea can still carry a punch.

1. Use Indian or Ceylonese tea.
2. Tea should be made in small quantities – that is, in a teapot. Tea out of an urn is always tasteless, while army tea, made in a cauldron, tastes of grease and whitewash.
3. The pot should be warmed beforehand.

4. The tea should be strong.
5. The tea should be put straight into the pot. No strainers, muslin bags or other devices to imprison the tea.
6. One should take the teapot to the kettle and not the other way about.
7. After making the tea, one should stir it, or better, give the pot a good shake, afterwards allowing the leaves to settle.
8. One should drink out of a good breakfast cup – that is, the cylindrical type of cup, not the flat, shallow type.
9. One should pour the cream off the milk before using it for tea.
10. One should pour tea into the cup first.
11. Lastly, tea – unless one is drinking it in the Russian style – should be drunk *without sugar*.

George Orwell's recipe for a perfect cup of tea,
Evening Standard, 12 January 1946

The great French philosopher Voltaire had his own ideas about the difference between France and England. France has many different kinds of sausage but one universal church, the Roman Catholic Church, he said. England, on the other hand, has many different varieties of church, but only *one sausage*.

Perhaps it is because the English survived centuries with one kind of sausage, which – sizzle as it might – looked much the same in the pan or out of it, they needed to provide variety some other way. Hence the variety provided by a dish called toad-in-the-hole.

Toad-in-the-hole is the quintessential English way of eating sausages, or originally bits of beef, all bunged in together to use up leftovers. As such, it was always a little class-conscious, as you might expect from an English dish. It was the kind of meal that even the wealthy rather enjoyed, even though it looked dangerously like a poor family's lunch – a 'homely yet savoury dish', according to the pioneer English cookery writer Mrs Beeton.

So it seemed to make polite sense to excuse the fact that even the wealthy rather liked it by calling it *traditional*. In fact, it stretches barely any further back in time than Voltaire himself. There it was on the menu of the Royal Philosophers, the Royal Society's Thursday evening dining club, eating in the Mitre Tavern in 1769, and there it was a few years later with an explanation: 'Baked Beef in Pudding, alias Toad in a Hole.'

It didn't satisfy everyone's need for class-conscious distinction. There was the novelist Fanny Burney describing the dish as 'ill-fitted' because it plunged a 'noble sirloin of beef into a poor paltry batter-pudding'.

The Mitre Tavern, once frequented by James Boswell and Samuel Johnson, was later pulled down to become a bank (it is now a pub again, because – as we know – English life goes in circles). The club moved down the Strand and carried on meeting for nearly a century. History doesn't relate how often they dined on toad-in-the-hole.

By then, the main ingredient of toad-in-the-hole had begun to mutate from any old bits of meat that happened to have been hanging around, into sausages. In the Second World War, frugal housewives were urged by the government to make it out of spam.

Yet there may have been a link with sausages right from the start, and that might explain the name. Because, there is some evidence about the origin of the nickname for this dish of kings and peasants. It seems to have derived originally from an Anglo-Saxon word, now slang, which sounds almost the same, a reference to the shape of the sausages. It seems to have been called *turd*-in-the-hole. I'm sorry, but it was.

Nigel Slater's classic recipe:

Set the oven at 220°C / gas mark 7. Whisk together 2 eggs and 300 ml of full-fat milk. Add a good pinch of salt, then beat in 125 g plain flour. Heat 3 tbsp of lard or dripping in a small roasting tin or baking dish until it starts to smoke. Add 6 fat pork sausages and let them colour on all sides then, while the oil and sausages are smoking hot, pour in the batter. Bake for 25–30 minutes until puffed and golden. Like making Yorkshire pudding, get the fat in the roasting tin (literally) smoking hot before adding the batter. I put the lightly cooked sausages in the pan first then pour in the batter when you can see a blue haze rising. I am a great believer in letting the batter rest before using, though others disagree.

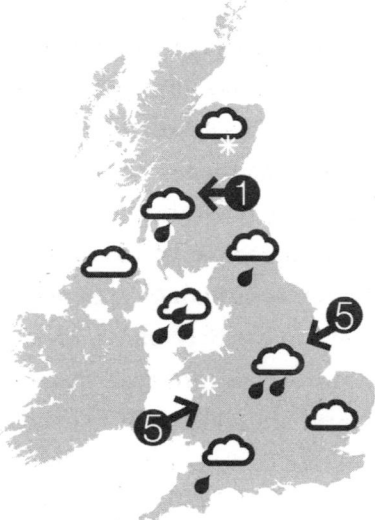

The man who speeded Charles Darwin to Tierra del Fuego, and fell out with him about the theory of evolution, fell victim in the end to the peculiar English relationship with the weather. Always far-sighted, Admiral Robert Fitzroy, as he was then, founded the first meteorological office, designed to warn shipping about imminent gales.

The office was enormously controversial. The shipowners found the whole idea intolerable because it meant that their vessels were, as they saw it, skulking in port – costing them money – when they could have been braving the weather on the high seas, delivering their cargo so that debts could be paid.

It was a tragic story. The shipowners lobbied for the funding to be withdrawn, Fitzroy's pioneering service was shut down and he cut his own throat in despair. The whole incident was a testament to the English obsession with weather and its wonderful unpredictability. Without unpredictable weather, after all, what would there be to talk about? When the great journalist Jerome K. Jerome set about describing the weather forecasts before his famous trip in *Three Men and a Boat*, it was their sheer inaccuracy that he was celebrating.

He described the smug attitude of those who listen to the forecasts and stayed in their digs on summer holiday, enjoying the fact that the other, less careful holidaymakers would be caught by the weather. 'Ah! they'll come in the afternoon, you'll find,' they said to each other. 'Oh, *won't* those people get wet. What a lark!' Jerome went on:

> And when the afternoon was nearly gone, and still there was no sign of rain, we tried to cheer ourselves up with the idea that it would come down all at once, just as the people had started for home, and were out of the reach of any shelter, and that they would thus get more drenched than ever. But not a drop ever fell, and it finished a grand day, and a lovely night after it.

There is the point about the English attitude to weather. They enjoy not knowing. Who wants to live somewhere where the weather is boringly predictable?

It is partly because of England's peculiar position. London is the same kind of latitude as Calgary in Canada, scene of the 1988 Winter Olympics, and of Irkutsk in Siberia, where they freeze dry the washing instantaneously and have to keep the car engines running all winter. In England, harsh winters are so unexpected that all the transport infrastructure immediately grinds to a halt and the schools close down. It is, of course, all to do with the benevolent Gulf Stream, which takes warm water and air from the Gulf of Mexico.

The weather determines English preferences for beer rather than wine because the climate isn't good for vines. Nor is all this rain good for dramatic geography – the biggest English canyon (Cheddar in Somerset) is three miles long (the Grand Canyon manages 227 miles). Swings and roundabouts.

You may find that the weather is far better than it is said to be. But please remember that the English don't heat their homes as much as other nationalities, so bring warm clothes.

Notice for new students at a language school in England

Once you know where to look for it, the evidence that wool once built England – the reason why successive Lord Chancellors have sat on a woolsack in the House of Lords since the fourteenth century – is all around us. The ruins of the great Cistercian abbeys that drove the production of fleece from the twelfth century onwards, the old drovers' roads that slice between fields and over hills and valleys, the vast wool churches, the songs – from 'Sheep May Safely Graze' to 'Little Boy Blue' – they are all testament that, once upon a time, England gave wool to the world.

Not to start with, of course. Southern Italy produced the best wool in the Dark Ages. But thanks partly to the Cistercian abbeys, with their distinctively white-robed monks – founding a distinctively English tradition of agrarian radicalism – it was English wool which crossed the Channel to the famous Champagne fairs, and from there went for cloth-making to Spain or Cyprus or Constantinople and beyond.

It was wool that drove the economic success of England, which in one generation – that of King Richard the Lionheart and his brother John – three times collected a quarter of the national wealth and sent it to Germany, while making barely a dent on the inflation that was such a by-product of success. The great sheep centres – Yorkshire, Gloucestershire and East Anglia – generated vast wealth for the growing nation in the centuries to come.

The Hundred Years War, which was primarily about getting access to Flemish weavers to create a home-grown industry to process the wool, deepened the relationship between the English and the wool trade. From 1275, the Great Custom, the tax on wool exports, was also a huge source of revenue for the English Crown.

By the fifteenth century, the textile trade had grown so much that exporting wool was forbidden. Smuggling it out of the country, a practice known as 'owling', meant losing a hand. The textile centres were then dominated by a radical system of cottage industries whereby the dyeing, weaving and finishing of products was distributed to people's homes and carried out domestically. This still continued until recently in the production of Harris Tweed, admittedly a Scottish brand. It was a system which broke the power of the guilds, but was in turn broken by the Industrial Revolution.

By that time the future of English wool was being overshadowed by the cotton industry, emerging more powerfully by then, and threatened also by the softer wool from Merino sheep bred and obsessively protected by the Spanish, which began to drive out the coarser English wool. By the twentieth century, the British textile industry was beset by underinvestment and monopolistic practices, and the writing was on the wall, as famous name after famous name shifted production overseas and then disappeared completely.

There then followed the global collapse in the use of wool – down forty per cent in 1966 alone – and the great relationship between England and the wool business, the source of their original wealth, was broken. A sad story, and rather typically English. Some English wool is used in carpets every year, but most of the rest – so laboriously sheared – just goes into incinerators or is exported to China for their carpets.

The relationship is broken, but traces remain, and so is the English romance with wool. There is a slow revival of the crafts industry that uses wool, and a handful of English producers who are bringing back the ancient English business of knitwear. There is a movement of amateur spinners and an even bigger movement of amateur knitters. The old tradition emerged most powerfully in recent years after Prince Charles intervened on behalf of the hill farmers and the wool industry – the fightback has begun.

I praise God and ever shall
It is the sheep hath paid for all.

Lines carved above a medieval
wool merchant's house

The phrase 'Bah! Humbug!' has long since passed into the English language, as a symbol of the mercantile approach to Christmas. It did so six days before Christmas in 1843, when Dickens published *A Christmas Carol*, at his own expense, and single-handedly reinvented an English Christmas – with roast turkey, families, presents, bonhomie and a very English kind of overindulgence.

Earlier that year, he had visited the Cornish tin mines and been appalled at the ragged children working there and planned a pamphlet, castigating their lack of education. In the end, he put the pamphlet aside and wrote the story instead and, by doing so, he turbo-charged its influence. The novella has ghosts and a whole series of Dickensian vignettes, lashings of nostalgia and a human transformation. In fact, *A Christmas Carol* is said to be one of the few books ever written that could genuinely change people's behaviour. Well into the twentieth century, the queen of Norway was still sending presents to poor children in London with a note saying 'With love from Tiny Tim'.

In fact, 1843 was rather an important year in the invention of an English Christmas. It was the first year where it can be proved that Christmas cards were sent. It was also three years after the arrival of Prince Albert, and the tradition of the Christmas tree arrived in England. A German-style Christmas was put back into what had become a rather dry, disapproving and puritanical nation, especially when it came to feast days, with their overtones of Catholicism.

But then, the English do live with the ghosts of Christmas Past, the exhaustion of Christmas Present and the fear of Christmas Yet to Come. They are not the only nationality to do so, but there is something overwrought and deliberately nostalgic about an English Christmas. Even the most sophisticated English professional, living in their Bauhuas white walls for 364 days a year, can still send Christmas cards with scenes of Dickensian mail coaches dashing through the snow. It is as if, on one day a year – perhaps a little longer – the history of England breaks through, and we pay our respects to it again. It is a period in the English psyche where transformation is possible.

The title of Dickens' book was deliberately chosen. It made the story sound mythic, ageless and reached back to the days when the English sang Christmas carols – and hastened the day when they would sing them again. But then, this may not have been Dickens' main intention when he wrote the book, though he carried on writing annual Christmas stories until 1849, when he was too busy with writing the great slab of *David Copperfield* to have time. His main intention was to extract a little generosity of spirit from the English in their most mercantile of moods.

And if we ever doubt that change is possible, a quick reread of *A Christmas Carol* can reassure us. There never was a transformation quite so instant as Scrooge's, but Dickens takes him through a process which makes it possible for us to have the same experience, part memory, part shame, part exorcism. As it is, he seems to have succeeded in resurrecting Merrie England from the bare, dry bones of utilitarianism and as such deserves the last place in this book – in the hope that someone might repeat the trick again some day soon.

But there is one final aside to be made about the Englishness of *A Christmas Carol*. In one sense, that is beyond dispute, it was so influential on the way the English live that it remade Englishness around it. Yet there is a peculiarity. The Cratchit family cooks a goose and enjoys it, but Scrooge wakes from his terrifying Christmas night and buys the prize turkey which has been hanging in the butchers, an exotic bird imported from America.

As a result, we have shunned the English goose and the English now almost universally eat American turkey. Bah! Humbug!

There never was such a goose. Bob said he didn't believe there ever was such a goose cooked. Its tenderness and flavour, size and cheapness, were the themes of universal admiration. Eked out by apple-sauce and mashed potatoes, it was a sufficient dinner for the whole family; indeed, as Mrs Cratchit said with great delight (surveying one small atom of a bone upon the dish), they hadn't ate it all at last! Yet every one had had enough, and the youngest Cratchits in particular, were steeped in sage and onion to the eyebrows!

Charles Dickens, A Christmas Carol *(1843)*

ACKNOWLEDGEMENTS

The idea for this book came to me in Monsal Dale walking with my wife Sarah, and I can't think of anyone better to talk about ideas while walking along a river with. If she hadn't been there, I'm not sure it would ever have seen the light of day. I'm ever so grateful to her for this and for so much else.

I would also like to thank my agent, Julian Alexander, for all his tireless advice and support. This book also wouldn't have happened without the imagination and hard work of the team at Square Peg, Caroline McArthur, Francesca Barrie, Rosemary Davidson, Mikaela Pedlow, David Milner, Matt Broughton, Simon Rhodes, Louise Court and Rachel Norridge.

I would also like to thank the following for permission to quote:

Bloomsbury International UK Ltd for permission to quote the series of apologies on page 11.

The Society of Authors as the Literary Representative of the Estate of John Masefield, for permission to quote from his poem 'Sea Fever' on page 71.

Helga Woodruff for permission to quote from William Woodruff's book *The Road to Nab End: An Extraordinary Northern Childhood*, on page 66. First published under the title *Billy Boy* by Ryburn Publishing Ltd in 1993. Republished by Eland Press in 2000, by Abacus in 2002, and by Eland Publishing Ltd in 2011. ISBN 9781906011260 Copyright © 1993 by Helga Woodruff, Copyright © 2008 by Asperula, LLC

The Society of Authors as the Literary Representative of the Alison Uttley Literary Property Trust for permission to use her recipe for Bakewell tarts on page 154.

Nigel Slater and Fourth Estate for permission to use his recipe for toad-in-the-hole on page 278.

'Middlesex' from Collected Poems by John Betjeman © The Estate of John Betjeman 1955, 1958, 1962, 1964, 1968, 1970, 1979, 1981, 1982, 2001.